MAKING AN IMPACT

BUILDING A TOP-PERFORMING ORGANIZATION FROM THE BOTTOM UP

MAKING AN IMPACT

BUILDING A TOP-PERFORMING ORGANIZATION FROM THE BOTTOM UP

Timm J. Esque

CEP Press
A wholly owned subsidiary of
The Center for Effective Performance, Inc.

Atlanta, Georgia

International
Society for
Performance
Improvement

For more information, contact:
CEP Press
2300 Peachford Rd.
Suite 2000
Atlanta, GA 30338
www.ceppress.com
(770) 458-4080 or (800) 558-4CEP

ISBN 1-879618-26-5

Library of Congress Catalog Card Number: 2001 131950

Printed in the United States of America

09 08 07 06 05 04 03 02 01 10 9 8 7 6 5 4 3 2 1

*This book is dedicated to
my daughter Jacquelin and
her generation.
May they usher in a new convention
of management.*

Contents

Acknowledgments

ONE OF THE COMMON SYMPTOMS OF INEFFECTIVE MANAGEMENT is inappropriate hero worship. Public recognition, bonus checks and plaques are showered on individuals and teams who "do whatever it takes" to recover from catastrophic problems. Meanwhile, individuals and teams who are competent enough to avoid those catastrophes in the first place are often ignored. There is nothing sexy about reliable performance. However, it is the key to long-term sustainable excellence. This book contains a number of case studies where leaders took a risk by implementing systems to ensure reliable performance. They didn't receive plaques or bonus checks or even thank you's for doing so. So I would like to thank just a few of them here. Thanks to Steve Cooper, Trish Dohren, Larry Gudis, Phil Lundberg, Greg Adkin, and Lee Benson—just a few of the true heroes of organizational performance.

William R. (Bill) Daniels not only provided the specifics for the case study for chapter 5, but has also been a valued mentor for many years. As I began my consulting business, I also received tremendous assistance and encouragement from Lila Sparks-Daniels, as well as Lila and Bill's team at American Consulting and Training. Don Tosti and Geary Rummler, two more giants in our field, provided much appreciated encouragement and ideas for this book. Denny Haywood, Sharon Shelton, Pierre Mourier and others provided comments from the perspective of my target audience. My friend and colleague Pat Patterson helped shape the final version of the manuscript, as did Vicki Chin and Suzanne Bennett at The Center for Effective Performance, Inc. (CEP), my partner in this project. Other people at CEP also provided valuable assistance: Ann Parkman, Seth Leibler, and Paula Alsher offered comments. Jill Russell provided editing, and Paige Harris and Samantha Gitlan handled operational and design issues.

Finally, I feel compelled to acknowledge Intel Corporation, my employer from 1983-1998. I have always believed that one of the reasons Intel has been so successful is because they are better than most at setting up the conditions for success that this book is all about. The methods in this book, especially chapters 3 and 4, were largely developed with Intel colleagues in Intel organizations.

Introduction

IN GENERAL, PEOPLE LIKE TO BE APPRECIATED BY OTHER PEOPLE. The same is true in organizations; members of an organization want to be valued by others in the organization for their contributions. As professions evolve, individuals in all fields strive to make a meaningful impact in the business world. Fifty years ago, the primary role of the Finance department was essentially the clerk role (Gup, 1987; Block and Hirt, 1989). The Finance department kept track of budgets and spending and conducted audits to see if reality matched "the books." Today, a large percentage of businesses are run by financial professionals, and virtually every large business has a chief financial officer or equivalent. Typical finance professionals today are in a consulting role either internal or external to their client organizations.

Although a relatively young profession, information technology has had a meteoric increase in responsibility in business organizations. The entire dot-com industry rests on the foundation of the information technology profession. And many chief technical officers have joined chief financial officers on executive staffs. Anyone who has ever been victim of a poorly timed system failure recognizes the value that an effective information technology function can bring to an organization.

But not all professions receive the same level of appreciation. Have you ever heard of a chief performance officer (CPO)? Are you and your training and performance colleagues viewed as consultants—respected members of the organization who are actively consulted before important performance-related decisions are made? Are you or your department held accountable for making measurable contributions to the bottom line? In my experience, the answer to these questions in most organizations is no. In my opinion, the training and performance profession has been under-appreciated in the business world.

One way that our profession has responded to this situation recently is by trying to unilaterally expand our responsibilities and contributions. We are attempting to re-engineer our role from that of training developer and deliverer, and occasional performance analyst, to the broader role of "performance improvement consultant" (or more commonly, performance consultant).

I am confident that our profession's ability to make an impact on organizations justifies this larger role and responsibility. But I am also concerned that we have not adjusted our practices sufficiently to warrant the new title of performance consultant. It is not clear to me that even our most talented performance analysts are yet appreciated enough by business organizations to be viewed and treated as consultants (at least not those operating internal to organizations). In fact, I believe there are some limitations inherent in the performance analyst role that could prevent training and performance professionals from being viewed like consultants rather than clerks.

The key question that faces our profession is: **What changes in our practices would enable us to impact the bottom line and be viewed by the larger organization as true and valued consultants? It is the premise of this book that by adjusting our own view of the performance consultant role, we can accomplish these things right now.**

A Note to All Managers

It is probably already obvious that the primary audience for this book is training and performance professionals. However, the systemic improvement of individual and organizational performance should be of interest to anyone in a leadership role. The few terms or concepts specific to the training and performance profession are usually explained as they arise. One exception is the term Human Performance Technology (HPT). HPT is a broad approach to solving individual and organizational performance problems that views performance as the product of many factors, including, but not limited to, performer knowledge and skills. In this book, I use HPT to refer to the ability to systematically consider and address the whole range of factors (e.g., clarity of goals, performance feedback, incentives, physical ability, knowledge and skills, etc.) that impact performance.

How to Use This Book

I've deliberately kept this book fairly short so that you can evaluate my answer to that key question with a relatively small investment on your part. At the end of the book, I've referenced a few select resources that can provide more of the specifics that you might desire if you decide that you are interested in learning more about this model of performance consulting. Whether you agree with my answer or not, I wish you (and your department, where applicable) the best of luck in becoming a more respected and appreciated part of your organization.

CHAPTER 1

MAKING AN IMPACT: AN ALTERNATIVE APPROACH

The Problem

A Parable

LONG AGO THERE WAS A POWERFUL KING ruling over a large kingdom. The king had advisors to help him make decisions, but mostly the advisors talked things over, looked concerned, and did as the king wished. When the king had serious problems (how to sack the next kingdom over, or how not to get sacked, for example), he would consult the oracle. The oracle never asked questions or discussed anything. It would listen to the king's complaint and, without hesitation, tell him what to do. The king usually followed the oracle's advice. Sometimes the king's troubles went away, and sometimes they didn't.

The king decided that the performance of this oracle was less than exemplary. His advisors agreed. Frustrated, the king asked his advisors to find a better oracle, one who could successfully solve the problems in the kingdom. The advisors set out to fulfill his request, and months later, the king was informed that a new oracle had been found (they had lured it with a lucrative benefits package). He went to the new oracle for advice on the latest problem. This oracle asked lots of questions. After interviewing the king and his advisors, the oracle then told the king that it would need time to collect more data and complete an analysis, and asked the king to return in two weeks. The king was leery, but obeyed.

When the king returned, the oracle presented a detailed proposal for addressing the king's problem. It even offered to head the effort to address the problem and complete an evaluation report. The king was happy enough to let the oracle take the problem off his hands, and agreed.

Three months later, the oracle reported back to the king: the effort had been successful. The king and his advisors were pleased. Another serious problem had arisen in the meantime so the king asked the oracle for additional help. Again there was data collection, analysis, implementation and a positive evaluation of the results. This cycle began to repeat itself. Every three to six months when a new problem occurred (or an old problem reappeared), the oracle would get involved. One snag after another was treated with the oracle's solutions and each was quite successful (as shown in the reports).

The oracle was quite busy, and decided it might be a good idea to look into getting some help with the workload.[1] Just about the time the oracle began searching for several assistants to keep up, our king and his kingdom were unfortunately sacked.

There are a number of lessons to this story, but the most important one is that **you cannot solve other people's or organization's problems *for* them (as the oracle was attempting to do) and expect a permanent solution.** People with lots of challenges and problems may want their problems solved for them, and they may even convince themselves that it can happen. In reality, though the problems may subside temporarily, they do not go away until the people who own them address them.

Don Tosti, a long-time successful performance consultant and expert on organizational culture, talks about this concept in a slightly different way (Tosti, 2000). He points out that taking on one isolated performance problem at a time is like throwing logs on a fire to keep the room warm. It works okay as long as someone is always present to throw on more logs (keep in mind that the client usually is trying to keep many "fires" going at the same time). But unless those fires are constantly fed, they will expire and the temperature will return to what it was originally. A more effective solution would be to install a thermostat—a system that continuously senses when temperatures are getting out of range and immediately initiates corrective action. The approach to performance consulting described in this book is very much like helping the king (or whoever *your* clients are) to install a thermostat.

The "log throwing" issue is relevant to all forms of organizational consulting. Yet as training and performance practitioners, we have another problem. Although we have a technology to help clients analyze and solve performance problems, unless we somehow attain the status of guru (or oracle), our clients generally will see us as advisors or support personnel who can only fulfill requests (e.g., "give me a training program"). Clients tend to have their own theories on human performance, and we are often viewed as simply offering "another opinion" on human performance issues. Many of us find ourselves in the position of aspiring to be successful at something (solving the client's performance problems for them) that we ultimately cannot succeed at and may not get the opportunity to do anyway.

Shoshana Zuboff, Harvard University social scientist and author, shed light on this problem in her presentation to over two thousand training and performance professionals at an International Society of Performance Improvement (ISPI) conference. Dr. Zuboff began by asking how many of the attendees saw themselves as performance improvement practitioners. At least 90 percent of the attendees raised their hands in response to this question. She then asked how many were encouraged in their current jobs to practice performance improvement (as opposed to training development and delivery, for example). This time only about a third of the hands were raised. Finally, she asked how many of those practitioners found it easy to get the opportunity to improve performance in their client organizations. Almost none of the two thousand people raised their hands.

Dr. Zuboff's conclusion was that certain chronic performance issues can never be solved in large established corporations (which were designed to support mass production). The opportunities for performance improvement lie primarily with organizations emerging in support of the new information economy, where new organizational designs can prevent old problems.

I offer an alternative. We can help *all* organizations systemically improve performance, but not by continuing to attempt to solve their problems for them. Instead, we can *and need* to **help performers and organizations learn to solve and prevent their own problems.**

This alternative approach:

- does not require that you be a guru to get an opportunity to practice,

- does not feel like following orders,

- allows you to draw on your expertise in Human Performance Technology (HPT),

- gets the client to systematically identify and solve his or her own problems, and

- results in improvements that are sustained over time.

The purpose of this book is to provide an overview of this alternative approach to performance consulting.

An Alternative Approach

What we are trying to avoid is approaching performance improvement from a reactive and fragmented stance. Rather than reacting to each isolated performance problem, the key to this approach is to make performance improvement integral to the way clients manage their work. After all, steering clear of problems, identifying problems that do arise early on, and resolving them so they do not occur again is what managing work is about. And every member of an organization, in some way, is responsible for managing work. Individual contributors are responsible for managing their own work (even if they and their managers don't realize it yet), others are responsible for managing work within a team or a function, others for managing across functions, and still others for managing entire organizations.

In its simplest form, managing work consists of three components:

- Setting goals;

- Letting work happen and comparing work completed against goals; and

- Deciding whether to change how the goals are being pursued.

When these three things are done well, individuals and organizations almost always meet goals. If they are not met, data is available to alter the goals before resources are wasted pursuing failure. People, teams and organizations who almost always hit their goals are successful. Hence, well-managed people, teams, and organizations will be successful.

Unfortunately, these three things are rarely done really well. All organizations exhibit some form of management behavior. Many organizations refer to these behaviors as "planning and control" and there are typically formal structures in place to make sure that they happen to some extent. For example, once organizations get to a certain size, they inevitably formalize a budgeting structure. This structure is intended to make sure that each part of the organization plans its activities and associated spending in accordance with a larger business plan. It includes "controls," such as signature authority and exception reports.

Yet despite existing planning and control mechanisms, few organizations prevent costly performance problems or ensure goals are consistently achieved at all levels of the organization. The mechanisms tend to fall short of accomplishing the three components of management (see figure 1.1 for a list of some common shortfalls). As a result, managers are frustrated and looking for something to make things better.

Enter the performance consultant. Anyone who really understands management and pays attention will easily gain credibility with clients, because he or she will be able to see how a client's emergency is simply a breakdown in these three components of management. With just a brief summary of the problem, the performance consultant can predict other symptoms and their impact on overall performance. There's no need to do a lengthy analysis before making a proposal, because when applying this approach the solution to performance problems is always the same. The solution is to help the person, team or organization manage itself more effectively. This begins by coaching them on a set of behaviors that they often know they should be doing, and probably are doing, just not very well. In other words, coaching them on setting goals, letting the work happen, comparing actual accomplishments to the goals, and making decisions about how to proceed. The consultant performing this role will be present when clients are deciding how to solve their own performance problems, and can take this opportunity to practice and share his or her Human Performance Technology (HPT) expertise.

Figure 1.1	Common Shortfalls of Existing Planning and Control Structures*
SHORTFALL	**DESCRIPTION**
Fuzzy Goals	Goals should be clear to everyone involved. A goal with any of the following deficiencies is a "fuzzy goal." • Stated in terms of behaviors or activities instead of accomplishments and outcomes. • Not specific in terms of the desired quantity or quality of the outcome. • Without clear individual owners, and/or not broken down to the individual level.
Conflicting Goals	To avoid conflicts, test goals for "alignment" as they are developed. Individual and team goals need to align with the next level up, and different teams' goals need to align with each other. If people believe their goals are in conflict with those of others, it is difficult to work together towards common objectives. Goals perceived as being in conflict effectively *are* in conflict.
Uninformed Decision Making	A key ongoing management decision is: "What will it take to stay on track to meet goals?" This decision must be influenced by recent past performance data (how actual performance has compared to planned performance). When accurate performance data is not available, not reviewed frequently, or not considered by management, the result is uninformed decisions.
Killing the Messenger	Organizations often believe that one way to prevent poor performance is to respond negatively when poor performance is reported. In reality, this stops the flow of accurate information, making informed decisions impossible. When people perceive that they may be punished for passing on what is going on in the trenches, they will find a way to stop passing on accurate performance data.
Over-design	Some overzealous team leaders or managers try to anticipate and address every possible obstacle before anyone is given a chance to perform. When work is over-designed, the actual performers have less ownership for and interest in their own success. Examples of over-design include detailed design of workstations, documentation and enforcement of detailed procedures, or mandatory training.

* Examples of planning and control structures include: budget structures, strategic planning cycles, annual/quarterly objectives, operations reviews, project progress reviews, and sometimes individual performance appraisal.

When clients have succeeded in learning the new behaviors, not only will the current emergency have gone away, but they will know how to address the next emergency. More importantly, they will know how to avoid most emergencies altogether, and they will see value in this. As a result, the performance consultant will feel and be valued. And that is a good place to be.

Peeling the Onion From the Inside Out

So how do you get to that place? Since all people are responsible for management to some extent, management will necessarily occur at all levels of an organization. The number of levels will vary from one organization to another, but each level requires all three components of management. This treatment of organizational levels is consistent with Rummler and Brache (1990). Now, think of these levels as layers of an onion. The outer layer of the onion is analogous to the uppermost tier of the organization, where organization-wide goals are set and monitored. At this layer, goals involve the overall direction of the organization and its highest business objectives, and decisions are large in scope.

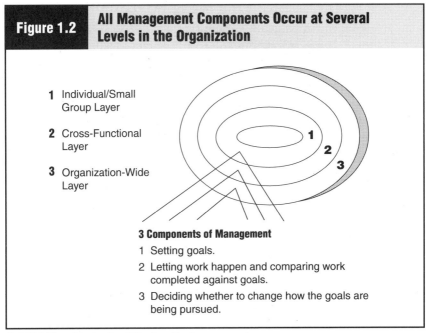

Figure 1.2	**All Management Components Occur at Several Levels in the Organization**

1 Individual/Small Group Layer

2 Cross-Functional Layer

3 Organization-Wide Layer

3 Components of Management
1 Setting goals.
2 Letting work happen and comparing work completed against goals.
3 Deciding whether to change how the goals are being pursued.

Below that layer is what might be called the cross-functional (or process and project) layer. The goals at this layer cover a smaller scope but must align with overall organizational goals. They include things like what products and services will be available when, and which internal processes currently need the most attention. Goals are reviewed and revised a little more frequently than at the higher layer. Peel this layer away and there is at least one more: the layer where individual and/or small group goals are set and monitored.

Because the three components of management are present at each "layer of the onion," performance consultants can begin practicing this approach to performance consulting at individual and small group levels and work their way up to the cross-functional and organization-wide levels. The same basic practices for helping an individual manage his or her work apply to helping an executive staff manage their organization's work. Of course, the magnitude of distractions and decisions are much greater at the executive level, so it is prudent to begin practicing this approach at the lower levels. This is what is meant by "peeling the onion from the inside out."

Peel away all the layers of an onion and you will be left with the very center, or pearl, of the onion. In this analogy, the pearl of the onion can be seen as commitment to goals. Commitment is often viewed as a rather "soft" factor of performance—difficult to influence and difficult to measure. But it doesn't have to be. In later chapters, we'll define commitment and discuss its position as an anchor to this alternative approach.

This book is organized to be consistent with peeling the onion from the inside out. The next chapter will describe how performance is managed at the individual and small group level, and how to begin consulting at this level. Chapters 3 and 4 broaden the scope to the level of work that cuts across teams and functional departments. Chapter 5 broadens the scope even further to the organization-wide level, where the primary clients are business managers who have responsibility for one or more profit centers. At the core of each chapter is a sequential flowchart for implementing this approach at each level of the organization and a detailed case study to illustrate the flowchart. The final chapter looks at the implications of this approach on the training and performance profession and our role in organizations.

It is common practice in "how-to" books to provide a summary of key content at the end of each chapter. In this book, chapters will end instead with a *Question and Answer* section. This section includes a few questions that I anticipated or that were asked by early reviewers of the book manuscript, along with my answers. This approach seemed more helpful in a book where the chapters are relatively short and certain issues are purposely not addressed in the main text, so as not to distract the reader from the key themes of the book.

Question and Answer

1. **How would I know for sure if the approach I use today amounts to "throwing logs on the fire"?**

What is most relevant is whether you are currently reaching your aspirations as a performance consultant. If not, here is a simple test for any approach you might be using today.

In your current approach…

1. who measures output/accomplishments of performers?

2. who is informed of the results of these measures?

3. who acts on these results?

If your answer to any of these three questions is NOT the client (and primarily the performers themselves) you are using something other than the "alternative" I've described.

2. **You claim that individual contributors manage their own work. Shouldn't management be the responsibility of managers?**

Although organizations have a tendency to define management as the things that managers do, the original notion of management is more specific. The first definition of "manage" in the *Random House Unabridged Dictionary (Second Edition)* is "to bring about or succeed in accomplishing, sometimes despite difficulty or hardship." Organizational accomplishments are the product of many individual accomplishments. Unless you believe it is management's responsibility to watch over individual contributors each hour of the day to make sure they are succeeding, then you must attribute some management responsibility to each individual. This is the concept of self-management or self-control that has been in management literature for at least forty years, but is misunderstood by many organizations. The consulting approach described in this book assumes that each individual contributor is responsible for self-management. Team leaders and managers are still necessary. For them, managing accomplishments is about coordinating accomplishments and information flow (planning, tracking and facilitating decisions) across groups, teams and whole organizations.

3. **Current approaches to performance consulting are based on the Human Performance Technology (HPT) framework. Is there a different framework for this alternative approach?**

The approach being described draws heavily on the HPT framework. In fact, some of the architects of HPT (Dale Brethower, Geary Rummler and others) were developing similar approaches and instructing business managers on them in the mid-1960's. (The course was called the Training Systems Workshop.) J.M. Juran, the quality improvement guru, also described and recommended many of the same concepts in his book, *Managerial Breakthrough* (1964).

Another framework that informs the approach described here is the self-control framework. Douglas McGregor's *The Human Side of Enterprise* (1960), provides an excellent example of this emphasis on self-control. Some more general but very relevant discussions of control and self-control that contribute to the approach in this book are in the following resources:

● "Managing for Breakthroughs in Productivity" by Allan Scherr. In *Human Resource Management*, 28 no. 3., 1989.

Question & Answer

- *Discovering Free Will and Personal Responsibility* by Joseph F. Rychlak. Oxford: Oxford University Press, 1979.

- *The Control Revolution: Technological and Economic Origins of the Information Society* by James R. Beniger. Cambridge: Harvard University Press, 1986.

- Chapter 6 of *Human Competence: Engineering Worthy Performance (Tribute Edition)* by Thomas F. Gilbert. Amherst, MA: HRD Press, 1996. Original edition, McGraw-Hill, 1978.

- *The Control Theory Manager* by William Glasser. New York: HarperCollins, 1994.

- "Feedback Systems" by William A. Deterline. In *Handbook of Human Performance Technology.* Edited by H.D. Stolovitch and E.J. Keeps. San Francisco: Jossey-Bass, 1992.

- Chapter 14 in *The Fifth Discipline: The Art and Practice of the Learning Organization* by Peter M. Senge. New York: Doubleday Currency, 1990.

- *The Human Use of Human Beings: Cybernetics and Society* by Norbert Weiner. Garden City, NY: Doubleday, 1954.

CHAPTER 2

WHERE TO BEGIN: INDIVIDUAL AND SMALL GROUP PERFORMANCE SYSTEMS

Towards a Self-Sustaining Performance System

THE DESIRED END RESULT when following this alternative approach to performance consulting is a Self-Sustaining Performance System (SPS). To implement all three components of management at any one of the three levels in an organization is to implement a Performance System (PS).[1] When most members at all levels of the organization are operating in an effective Performance System most of the time, we have helped our client implement a Self-Sustaining Performance System.

Self-Sustaining Performance Systems have been implemented successfully from the bottom up, from the top down and even from the middle out. As promised in the previous chapter, we'll begin with PS implementation at the individual/small group level, where grasping and practicing the approach is simplest.

The simplest way to think about a Performance System is that it consists of the three components of management stated in terms of the desired conditions for each individual performer:

1. the performer knows what he is expected to produce in order to be successful;

2. the performer generates his own frequent feedback about whether he is being successful; and

3. the performer knows that if he provides warning that he is not succeeding, the response from management will be to help him succeed or to change the expectation.

Bill Daniels, author and long-time practitioner of this approach, summarizes these three conditions as clear expectations, frequent self-monitored feedback and control of resources (1995). Consulting at the individual/small group level begins by finding out if the performer is already operating in the three PS conditions, and if not, implementing the first two conditions: clear expectations and frequent self-monitored feedback. Because the first condition involves clarifying and usually quantifying the performer's desired output, measuring the change in performance from before and after PS implementation is simple. Implementing the first two PS conditions typically results in performer productivity increases of 30 percent or more in a very short time (Feeney, 1973; Daniels, 1995; Esque, 1996). As you can imagine, being able to document these types of results in the short-term builds the credibility of the performance consultant. This is by no means a bad thing, but a Performance System is primarily focused on longer-term sustainable improvements in performance. The medium- and long-term impact of the PS comes into play with the third condition: control of resources.

After several weeks of performing in a work situation where the first two conditions are present, most people know both what they are capable of producing and what is limiting that capability. This is the perfect time to ask the performers: a) what would most help you increase your production capability? and b) how much more productive would you be if your requests were fulfilled? These are essentially the same questions all performance consultants attempt to answer, but having the performers address these questions directly is an important feature of this consulting approach. Keeping the performers (and their managers) in the "driver's seat" ensures they maintain ownership of both problems and solutions. As a result, they will tend to do whatever it takes to ensure that *their* clearly stated performance goals are achieved, including fully utilizing the performance consultant. By answering the key questions themselves and presenting their case to management, the performers develop a sense of control over the resources needed to accomplish current and future goals.

A Vision of Success: A Small Group Performance System in Action

The ultimate goal of performance consulting should be clients who can sustain excellent performance with less and less help. The longest-running small group Performance System I've ever witnessed had no direct consulting support at all. What it had was a compelling need to succeed and one day of training on Performance Systems. This particular team operated in an effective PS for at least five years, during which it boosted its own revenues from just under $200 thousand per year to well over $1 million and had very little turnover. People were basically lobbying to get into this organization.

The group was created within a large company to provide computer board repair service for a factory full of computer driven machinery. Factory floor technicians swapped good boards for bad ones out of the machines, and these boards were then sent to the 15 (approximately) board repair technicians to be fixed. In order to become permanent, the group needed to pay for itself eventually. It needed to be more convenient *and* cost-effective to repair the boards in-house, rather than sending them out for repair.

The manager educated his team on what this meant in terms of productivity, including understanding the exact cost burden on the factory, and therefore, how many boards per month needed to be serviced in order for cost savings to exceed actual costs. He then placed a white board in the most visible part of the lab for tracking weekly boards repaired, and weekly revenue (costs saved by staying in-house) against the cost burden. At the end of each day, the technicians tallied their accomplishments and added them to the weekly total. Each individual technician knew how many boards he needed to complete each week in order to achieve the overall small group goals. Individual boards completed were tracked in the formal log, so that anyone could see what was being accomplished by whom any time.

Bi-monthly, the manager led "control of resources" meetings in which the entire team reviewed recent performance against goals and discussed ways in which they could improve. The manager was the ultimate decision maker, but he had created an environment in which everyone felt safe and wanted to participate. The group's recommendations were usually sound, and he had no problem supporting them. After a couple of years, the group had become so efficient that they either needed to service more factories or shrink their headcount. The manager found more business, and as a result, the group stayed about the same size during the five years I observed it. A few technicians left for personal reasons, but there were always more anxious to join the group.

This group had the joint benefits of small size and clear success criteria. But even under similar conditions, few groups perform this well for this long. Individuals and groups embedded in a larger organization can often encounter difficulties due to fuzzy or conflicting goals or team leaders and managers failing to understand the importance of accurate performance data. There is a tremendous opportunity for performance consultants to help their clients follow this example of a successful PS. The remainder of this chapter provides a detailed example of implementation at the individual/small group level. Figure 2.1 illustrates the eight sequential steps of PS implementation at this level and gives an objective for each step. The following case study illustrates the eight steps.

Individual and Small Group PS Implementation: A Case Study

This example involves an engineering and machine shop with under 100 employees that repairs worn aircraft parts for airlines and other aircraft operators. The main shop was organized into three functional areas or small groups: machining, electroplating, and assembly tear-down and overhaul. The typical "job" moved through two or more of these functional areas one or more times before it was complete. The company was already quite successful, having grown from less than $500 thousand to about $4 million dollars in revenue over the previous four years. The company was planning to implement a new shop floor tracking system and asked the performance consultant for help to make sure the system provided the information most useful to production management.

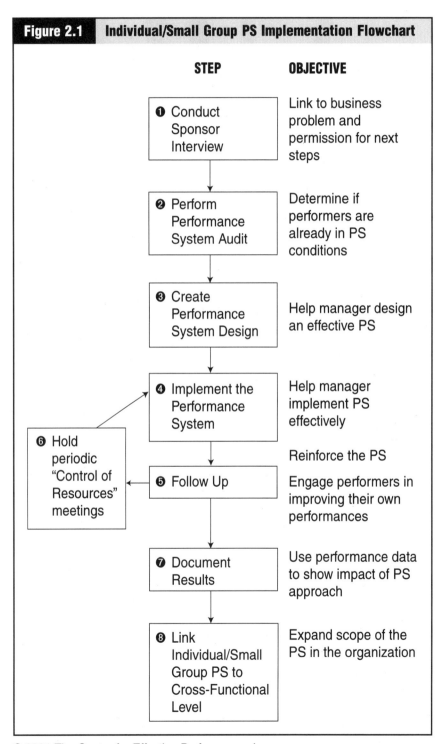

Figure 2.1   **Individual/Small Group PS Implementation Flowchart**

STEP	OBJECTIVE
❶ Conduct Sponsor Interview	Link to business problem and permission for next steps
❷ Perform Performance System Audit	Determine if performers are already in PS conditions
❸ Create Performance System Design	Help manager design an effective PS
❹ Implement the Performance System	Help manager implement PS effectively
❻ Hold periodic "Control of Resources" meetings	Reinforce the PS
❺ Follow Up	Engage performers in improving their own performances
❼ Document Results	Use performance data to show impact of PS approach
❽ Link Individual/Small Group PS to Cross-Functional Level	Expand scope of the PS in the organization

Step 1. Conduct Sponsor Interview

OBJECTIVE: Link to the business problem and get permission for next steps.

The sponsor in this case was the president of the company. In the conversation about the new shop floor tracking system, the consultant asked the president how the people doing the work (the technicians) would use the new system. The president said the technicians would enter data into the system, but would not typically use system output (reports, etc). Instead, he believed that technicians would get the information they needed from the supervisors. This raised a flag for the consultant; performers often aren't fully productive because they do not have the information they need (their actual performance compared to clear expectations). At the consultant's urging, the president agreed that while the consultant was collecting data, it wouldn't hurt to find out if the technicians were getting the information they needed throughout the work day (to determine if they were working in PS conditions). In a follow-up meeting, the consultant obtained approval for a data collection proposal that included a PS audit. The consultant also met the production management team, who promised their cooperation in data collection.

Step 2. Perform Performance System Audit

OBJECTIVE: Determine if performers are already in PS conditions.

The PS audit is an easy way to find out if performers are working in PS conditions. Figure 2.2 shows the simple audit form used to collect data from several performers from each functional area. The consultant conducted brief interviews (three to seven minutes) with the technicians at their work stations. The consultant also asked area supervisors similar questions to get their perceptions of how information was currently provided to the technicians. Typical patterns emerged quickly. Of 25 technicians surveyed, not one knew exactly what he or she was expected to produce that day. Only one out of 25 had a way of tracking his or her own daily output, and most of the rest believed that because each job was different, tracking individual output wouldn't make much sense.

In the current situation, every day began with an area meeting in which each technician was assigned "job steps." A job step was the term used to

FIGURE 2.2	Example Performance System Audit Form

Employee Survey

Name: _____ Area: _____

Summaries published by area if appropriate; individual responses confidential.

1. Where does your finished work go from here?

2. Do you have a goal for the week? If yes, what is it?

3. Do you have a goal for today? If yes, what is it?

(Interviewer Note: If the answers to questions 2 & 3 are "no," the interview is over.)

4. Is that what your supervisor expects also?

5. Do you think you will hit your goal today?

    How do you know?

6. What will you do if you discover you can't finish today?

7. What do you do when you make it with plenty of time to spare?

describe the work to be done on a specific job in a specific area, such as electroplating. When a technician completed an assignment or got stuck, he or she needed a supervisor's instructions to decide what to do next. This type of task-to-task planning (or lack of planning) is typical in organizations that are responding to jobs that are furthest behind, rather than preventing jobs from falling behind. Organizations that operate this way will, predictably, have difficulty staying on schedule. In this organization, the formal schedule measurement (business indicator) was on-time delivery, measured as the percentage of jobs completed and delivered by the customer request date. Recent on-time delivery was averaging below 60 percent. From management interviews, it was apparent they believed performance was somewhere around 70 percent and that was okay, considering they let the customer set delivery dates (rather than negotiating more realistic ones). However, when the actual data was presented to the management team (including the interviewees), along with the evidence that technicians were operating without goals, they agreed unanimously that an effort must be made to improve their delivery performance.

Step 3. Create Performance System Design

OBJECTIVE: Help manager design an effective PS.

Beginning the following week, supervisors would help each technician plan a full day's work each morning. The objective was not to pile more work on the technicians but to set them up to be productive all day, rather than one task at a time. This change also required the supervisors to plan further ahead and focus on keeping *all* jobs moving, not just jobs critical to the current week's schedule.

In addition to the change in goal-setting, the technicians needed a way to generate feedback on their own performance. Feedback systems can be designed with participation from the performers, by the supervisors themselves, or with guidance from the performance consultant; just remember that those who feel ownership for the feedback system will be more intent on seeing that it succeeds. In this particular application, each supervisor designed the feedback system for his own area after the consultant presented several possibilities. Once the consultant had a chance to review each design and suggest refinements, the supervisors presented the new goal-setting and feedback approach to their respective functions.

Step 4. Implement the Performance System

OBJECTIVE: Help manager implement the PS effectively.

In this case, the feedback system took the form of individual performance tracking sheets (see one example in figure 2.3). The sheets varied for each functional area, but in each case, technicians were to use the sheets to track what they accomplished each day against what they had planned to accomplish.

In the tracking sheet example shown, goals were set in terms of a specified number of job steps for each two-hour block. Although supervisors had final say on each technician's daily goal, they were instructed to get technician input before finalizing goals. When done properly, this solidifies performer commitment to the goals (the "pearl in the onion"), which is

FIGURE 2.3	**Example Individual Performance Tracking Sheet**								

Daily Tracking Sheet for: _____ Week of: _____

	Monday		Tuesday		Wednesday		Thursday		Friday	
Number of Job Steps	Plan	Complete	Plan	Complete	Plan	Complete	Plan	Complete	Plan	Complete
First 2 hours	1	/	0	/	2	/				
Second 2 hours	3	///	3	//	2	////				
Third 2 hours	3	//	3	//	2	////				
Fourth 2 hours	2	//	2		2	//				
Total	**9**	**8**	**8**	**5**	**8**	**11**				
Percent	**89%**		**63%**		**138%**					

Note: To achieve a small group PS each individual needs to be operating in the three PS conditions. In this example, small groups of technicians performing like tasks shared the same PS design, but each individual performer used the PS design to track his or her own performance. Hence the term individual/small group PS.

critical to long-term success. The technicians recorded the goals on their tracking sheets and monitored when they completed work on specific job steps. The goals for each two-hour period varied somewhat depending on the nature of specific jobs, availability of workstations, and other non-production tasks for which the technicians were responsible.

Step 5. Follow Up

OBJECTIVE: Reinforce the PS.

A critical component of the PS is frequent supervisor follow-up. Supervisors were instructed to check in with technicians once or twice a day to recognize completed work and be available if technicians needed help or specific resources to complete any part of their goals. The supervisors were advised *not* to point out when someone was behind, since performers working in PS conditions already know if they are not being successful.

Part of the consultant's role at this stage is to follow up with supervisors to ensure *they* are following up with performers. It is sometimes a good idea to check with performers as well to make sure they are getting the appropriate messages from supervisors. In this particular case, two of the three areas got off to an excellent start. The third area was undergoing a supervisor change and implemented daily goal setting but did not implement individual tracking sheets at that time. It is the consultant's responsibility to point out when the approach is not being adhered to, but the sponsor must choose whether to take action on these observations.

Step 6. Hold Periodic "Control of Resources" Meetings

OBJECTIVE: Engage the performers in improving their own performance.

This company was already holding periodic meetings to get technician input into procedural improvements, but as is often the case, they were missing key performance data. The consultant encouraged supervisors to begin area improvement meetings with the performance data that the technicians were generating. White boards were set up in each area to track the total work completed each day, based on the individual tracking sheets (though it's important to note that these boards only showed a summary and were not used to compare individual performances against each other). The area meetings now began with recent performance data and a few questions:

- Are we successfully meeting our area goals each week?

- If not, what will it take to be able to achieve those goals?

- If so, are we ready to increase our goals and still reliably achieve them?

- What will it take to do that?

This changed the structure of area meetings from brainstorming improvements to determining what it would take for technicians to have control over resources required to meet goals. One of the first lessons learned was that the first two hours of the day were usually much less productive than the others. Based on this new knowledge, the initial "control of resources" meeting discussions focused on how to get rolling more quickly each morning.

These "control of resources" meetings are a great opportunity for the consultant to educate the client on effective performance analysis and possibly do some analysis as modeling. Because the analysis is based on the performers' own data and because they are participating heavily in the improvement process, they will be fully invested in implementing the improvements. When the performers think a change is a good idea, the battle is halfway won, and in fact, under these circumstances, change may not seem like a battle at all!

Step 7. Document Results

OBJECTIVE: Use performance data to show the impact of the PS approach.

During the initial management meetings (after the data collection), managers determined that the primary measure of success for this intervention was on-time delivery. This was ideal because it was already being measured, it was considered key to overall company success, and there was room for improvement (even though management had seemed satisfied prior to the intervention). On-time delivery performance, the results of which were posted in the company cafeteria, began improving almost immediately after implementing the goal-setting and tracking sheets.

Figure 2.4 shows the average monthly on-time delivery (as a percentage of total jobs scheduled) before and after the intervention.

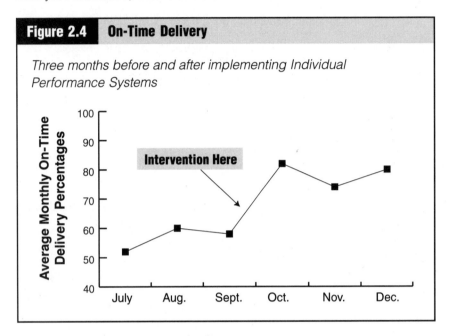

Figure 2.4   On-Time Delivery

Three months before and after implementing Individual Performance Systems

Step 8. Link Individual/Small Group PS to Cross-Functional Level

OBJECTIVE: Expand the scope of the PS in the organization.

Nothing is more effective in convincing a sponsor to expand a PS to the next level than positive data from the initial intervention. In this case, the next logical step was to elevate the intervention to the cross-functional or process level. At the process level, improvements would be coordinated across the three functional areas (machining, electroplating, and assembly tear-down and overhaul) to systematically identify each bottleneck in the overall repair and production process.

The next chapter introduces the implementation of a Performance System at the cross-functional level of an organization and provides a separate case in which a PS improved the performance of a cross-functional process.

The

Question & Answer

1. If the three conditions of a Performance System reflect the three components of management, is every management system a Performance System?

Yes and no. A PS *is* a management system. But as discussed in chapter 1, many supposed management (planning and control) systems are missing components or suffer from poor execution of one or more components. Even a complete management system may fall short of the demands of an organization operating in a specific environment. So, to be more specific, a PS is a class of management system designed to meet the needs of today's fast-paced and dynamic organizations.

2. If the company in the second example was successfully growing, why would they be seeking performance consulting?

Clients are not likely to call in a performance consultant specifically to overhaul their day-to-day management system. The opportunity to implement a PS almost always begins with a conversation about some other specific performance problem or opportunity. In this case, it began with the sponsor seeking assistance implementing a new shop floor tracking system. The PS was then presented to the sponsor as a chance to improve the business goal of on-time delivery, not as a PS opportunity. This case helps to demonstrate the range of requests for help that can be turned into PS implementations. Though total quality management and open-book management principles had already helped to create a more successful organization, from a PS perspective, there was still a large potential for improvement. In my experience, relatively successful organizations are the ones most likely to seek out and be open to additional help.

3. When you say managers "helped" the technicians plan a full day's work, who had final say in setting the technician's daily goals?

Managers can only be sure that a performer is committed when he or she agrees to goals without coercion. There are times when it is appropriate for managers to establish a goal without performer agreement (such as when the manager has much more experience with the tasks than the performer), but that is the exception.

A commitment is when a specific performer agrees to produce specific deliverables, to specific quality criteria, at a specific time. When performers do commit to performance goals and then generate their own performance feedback, they can be counted on to meet their commitments or provide advance warning if they fall behind.

4. Can you design a feedback system for work that is creative in nature and harder to measure? Why aren't there more examples of different feedback system designs?

Setting clear expectations and providing frequent feedback for creative work or knowledge work is a little more challenging than for straightforward production work. However, as much as some performers would like to believe their work cannot be measured, nearly all work can. Performers who can accurately estimate how much work they can complete in a given time are much more valuable than performers who cannot. Part of the art of PS design and implementation is helping performers and their managers turn nebulous work into discrete accomplishments.

No matter how much instruction and how many examples are provided on feedback system design, there will always be more questions about specific situations. Chapters 3 and 4 provide a couple more examples of feedback system design. See also the first two references listed on page 106 (Daniels, 1995 and Esque, 1999).

CHAPTER 3

ACROSS THE BOARD: SYSTEMS FOR PROCESS MANAGEMENT

The Pipeline of the Organization

INDIVIDUAL PERFORMANCE SYSTEMS ARE THE FOUNDATION of a Self-Sustaining Performance System. But in today's complex world, very few finished products or services are produced by one individual. As a result, the key performance challenges for most organizations revolve around effectively coordinating work across individuals, sub-teams and departments.

When a group of individuals, sub-teams or departments come together *temporarily* to produce a specific outcome, we call it a "project." Projects are used to construct or renovate buildings and factories, to develop new products and services, to create or revise information systems, etc. Other interdependent groups form to sustain *ongoing* "processes." Examples of processes include: production lines, customer service centers, sales and distribution centers, etc. The next two chapters will focus on implementing Performance Systems in processes and projects, as well as linking them to the individual level.

The vast majority of the time that organizations are looking for help with performance improvement, they are looking for help with their processes and projects. After all, this is where most work takes place, and it is where the most important work takes place. An organization's processes and projects are what bring products and services to the customer; they are the pipeline of the organization. Without this ability, most organizations would have no reason for existing.

That said, very few organizations manage processes or projects really well. It is one thing for a group of people all working under the same charter (in the same department, for example) to reach some semblance of a shared purpose. It is quite another thing to achieve and sustain a shared purpose across team, departmental and other organizational barriers. This is a big part of what Geary Rummler and Alan Brache were referring to in the title of their seminal book: *Improving Performance: How to Manage the White Space on the Organization Chart* (1990).[1] How can organizations ensure that each member of a process or project is working with clear expectations and frequent feedback, and that the expectations and feedback are aligned with the desired outputs of the larger process/project?

A crucial factor for effective consulting at this cross-functional level in the organization is the practicality of the approach. There are an unlimited and growing number of tools, methods and approaches for assisting process and project performance. But how many add more value in terms of sustainable improved performance than they cost in the time spent learning, promoting and implementing them? This is where the PS has a huge advantage over many others because it builds on a structure (planning and control) that to some extent already exists in every organization.

To Tweak or Not to Tweak: Underlying Principles for Process Management

Most process improvement work today derives from the "total quality" movement. Total quality began with a focus on applying statistics to concrete and often complex processes, such as various types of assembly lines (Butman, 1997). Statistical process control charts are still used today, especially in the most complex manufacturing environments. But the most common form of process improvement is probably process redesign.

While statistical process control is especially useful for controlling the mechanized aspects of a process, process redesign is usually more focused on the human aspects. Steps in a process are mapped out and the relationships between steps are analyzed to identify disconnects and inefficiencies. Specific steps are also sometimes identified as barriers to successful performance, and root cause analysis or cycle time reduction may be used to "fix" those steps. As you might guess, the application of Performance Systems to processes is more analogous to process redesign than statistical process control. However, to achieve a process-oriented Performance System, process redesign must be based on two of the key principles that underlie statistical process control. The following story demonstrates these principles.

It seems safe to assume that the vast majority of large manufacturing companies have by now implemented or attempted to implement some form of total quality management in their factories. Unfortunately, many of these companies approached total quality more as a program than as a philosophy. Members of an organization must believe that improving quality simultaneously improves productivity to reap the full benefits of the total quality toolset. I was lucky enough to be in one such company in the late 1980s, when the quality movement was in its heyday. I was working in a state of the art computer chip factory at the time and experienced the implementation of total quality management first hand.

The process of manufacturing computer chips is called wafer fabrication. Integrated circuits are produced on thin "wafers" of silicon that eventually are sawed into many individual chips and packaged for distribution. The process for producing the integrated circuits is complex, usually involving a hundred or more separate operations. At each stage there is a high potential for "killing" one or more of the chips on each wafer. The goal is to lose as few individual chips as possible throughout the production line. The "yield" refers to the percentage of good chips compared to the total potential chips on a wafer.

In the factory where I worked in 1986, the people responsible for the yield of good chips were the Process Engineers (PE's). There were about 30 PE's divided across specific portions of the production line, and each PE was in charge of improving the yield on two to five process steps in the same functional area. PE's spent their days making calculated "tweaks" and measuring the local impact. Their success was measured in terms of the yield of chips as wafers passed through their portion of the process.

When statistical process control charts first appeared, the first thing I noticed was the difficulty the implementers had in getting past the first step. Paradoxically, the first step towards process control and improvement is to stop making improvements to the process: to stop tweaking. PE's had been hired to tweak, they were rewarded for tweaking, and as far as I could tell, they enjoyed tweaking. But until you stop tweaking a process, it is impossible to determine its current capability. And until that is determined it is impossible to establish control limits.

After several months, the current capability for key processes had still not been established, and a decision was made to greatly reduce the number of PE's. The remaining PE's became consultants to the manufacturing supervisors, instead of being responsible for yield. This was a tremendous change to the organizational chart and the culture of the fabrication plant. It also worked. A few months after this change, control charts had been successfully installed, and systemic improvement had begun. The company built on this success and became a world-class computer chip manufacturer within a few years.

This experience with process improvement illustrated the two key principles mentioned earlier. First, in order to improve a process, you have to leave it alone long enough to understand the current process performance. Second, it is critical that improvement is done incrementally and in a coordinated fashion. If improvements are made simultaneously throughout the process (as they had been previously in this case), there is no way to determine the impact of any one improvement on the overall results. And when you don't understand why a process is improving or declining, it is very difficult to sustain improvement over any period of time. These principles are undoubtedly prerequisite to effective statistical process control, and they are just as important for the less mechanistic process redesign. Process redesign approaches that do not heed these principles are doomed to short-term improvement at best, and wasted effort and energy at worst.

Because of these two principles, I prefer the term "process management" to process improvement or continuous improvement. Lots of organizations already practice process improvement and continuous improvement (in the form of lots of uncoordinated tweaking), but relatively few have yet mastered process management. The process-oriented PS is an excellent vehicle for effective process management. Effective process management begins not with "process redesign" but rather with "process clarification." Process clarification is the term I use for involving the process contributors in understanding the current capability of their process before any improvement begins. With these clarifications in terminology, let's turn now to an example. The flowchart in figure 3.1 illustrates the seven sequential steps of PS implementation at the process level and the objective for each step. The following example then illustrates the seven steps.

Figure 3.1	Process-Oriented Performance System Implementation Flowchart

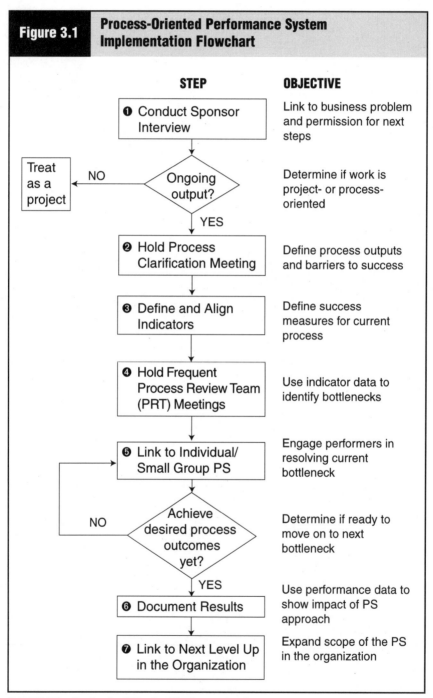

© 2001 The Center for Effective Performance, Inc.

Process-Oriented Performance System Implementation: A Case Study

Raven University* is a private educational institution offering both degree and non-degree programs. The university has been successful both as an educational institution and as a business, but by late 1998, problems in its accounts receivable process were apparent. The two primary measures of success of this process were total accounts receivables (AR) and the percentage of total AR over 90 days old. Both of these measures had been trending upwards substantially and disproportionate to growth in university enrollment, and the university felt that something needed to be done to get AR back in control.

Step 1. Conduct Sponsor Interview

OBJECTIVES: Link to the business problem and get permission for next steps. Determine if work is project- or process-oriented.

In the sponsor interview, the campus head presented the problem to the consultant as twofold. First, there was clearly a problem in the Accounting department. Secondly, the primary strategy for the university to date had been rapid growth, and the sponsor felt it was probably time to focus on process improvement in general. True process problems are never isolated to just one participating function, and predictably, during the interview it became apparent that Accounting was not the only department that impacted AR. In fact, collecting payment was the last step in the university's core process of enrolling new students, providing them with quality education, and providing substantial administrative support (which happened to include processing payments).

The consultant presented a proposal consistent with the PS flowchart in figure 3.1, and also suggested a re-positioning of the business problem. Calling the target process the "enrollment-to-payment" process helped clarify that several departments in addition to Accounting were involved with the process, and that it would take cooperation from all those departments to achieve success. The consultant positioned the intervention not as process improvement but rather as ongoing process management,

---

* Name has been changed.

beginning with process clarification. The sponsor accepted the proposal and scheduled a process clarification meeting.

Step 2. Hold Process Clarification Meeting

OBJECTIVE: Define process outputs and barriers to success.

Prior to the actual process clarification meeting, the managers of all departments involved in the enrollment-to-payment process met. The purpose of this meeting was to inform the leadership about the larger intervention and the upcoming process clarification meeting, as well as to get agreement on the ultimate desired outcome of the target process. It was determined that in addition to keeping AR at manageable levels, the process also needed to maintain a consistently high-quality education for the students and continued growth in enrollment. At the time, both educational quality and enrollment levels were on track, so department managers agreed that emphasis should be put on reducing AR without negatively impacting the other two outcomes.

The process clarification meeting was a full day meeting with about 50 participants, representing the 250 or so people who contributed to the enrollment-to-payment process on a day-to-day basis (mostly individual contributors, representing all functions that contributed to the process). After a presentation explaining the business problem and clarification of the ultimate desired result of the process, the participants worked through several structured exercises to clarify the existing process. The meeting followed the recommended process clarification agenda shown in figure 3.2. The role of the consultant was to coach management on setting up the meeting and then facilitate the meeting according to the objectives and agenda.

During the meeting, participants realized that the Accounting department was set up for failure. For example, because Enrollment was the driver for growth and profitability, they tended to leave the discussion of payment and payment options to other administrative functions. Administrative Services, on the other hand, assumed payment options were discussed and solidified during enrollment. The sub-process for financial aid was understaffed, causing accounts receivable to "age" before AR personnel even became involved (the older the AR, the less chance of collecting, hence the measure of the percentage of total AR over 90 days old). And in an effort to satisfy the university students, financial services

Figure 3.2	Recommended Process Clarification Meeting Agenda		
ITEM	**ACTIVITY**	**OUTCOME**	**EST. TIME**
1	Sponsor Presentation	Clarity on ultimate process outcomes and success measures.	10 min.
2	Housekeeping Warm-Up Activity Meeting Agenda/Roles Ground Rules	Clear expectations for this meeting.	50 min.
3	Define Functional Inputs and Outputs	What each functional team contributes to the process, and the inputs they need from other functions to succeed.	60 min.
4	Validate the Output Matrix	Rough process sequence of events. Clarification of ownership.	90 min.
5	Define Quality Requirements for Key Outputs	Criteria for each internal deliverable.	60 min.
6	Prioritize Barriers to Success	Determine if there are any "low hanging fruit" barriers to success.	60 min.
7	Next Steps	Quick description of indicator development and review. Form the Process Review Team.	30 min.
8	Wrap Up	Issues turned into actions, and expectations about what the team will do with meeting outcomes.	30 min.

© 2001 The Center for Effective Performance, Inc.

personnel were frequently waiving fees and university policies, making it very difficult to stick to the policies on the payment collection end of the process.

Again, at least two of these problems were predictable. The front end of these "pipeline" processes usually have to do with generating business. In the effort to attract new business, promises are often made to customers that are difficult, if not impossible, to meet later on. Another reason customer expectations aren't met is because the most labor-intensive resources are often constrained in an effort to manage costs. It's not too difficult to predict a disconnect when customers are told anything is possible, but resource allocation is structured to keep the organization mean and lean. Yet if each department is managing itself independently to optimize performance against its own goals, leaders of the organization may not recognize the impending conflict.

Once participants clarified process outputs and identified the top few barriers to overall performance, they agreed to continue implementing a PS (per the flowchart). A "process review team" (PRT) was formed to drive the rest of the intervention. The PRT was made up of one or two representatives from all functions involved in the enrollment-to-payment process, including both supervisors and individual contributors. This team would make sure that all functions managed themselves to optimize performance against the desired outcomes of the process. Their first job was to establish, *with data*, that the issues identified in the process clarification meeting were in fact the ones preventing overall success.

Step 3. Define and Align Indicators

OBJECTIVE: Define success measures for current process.

In the process clarification meeting, participants agreed on what each functional group would need to produce (outputs) in order to support the ultimate desired outcome (see output-based process flowchart in figure 3.3). Although Enrollment benefited in the short-term by setting attractive expectations for the customer, they agreed that to support the larger process they needed to encourage more realistic expectations. This meant that in addition to producing "newly enrolled students," they also needed to produce a form signed by each new student which indicated an understanding of the payment obligation and a chosen method of payment (e.g., cash, corporate reimbursement, financial aid, etc.). The production

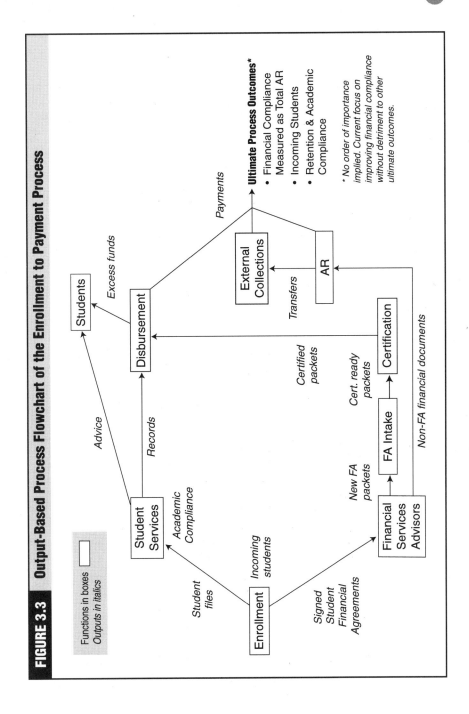

FIGURE 3.3   Output-Based Process Flowchart of the Enrollment to Payment Process

Functions in boxes
Outputs in italics

Enrollment

Student files

Incoming students

Signed Student Financial Agreements

Student Services

Academic Compliance

Advice

Records

Disbursement

Excess funds

Students

Financial Services Advisors

New FA packets

Non-FA financial documents

FA Intake

Cert. ready packets

Certification

Certified packets

AR

Transfers

External Collections

Payments

Ultimate Process Outcomes*
* Financial Compliance Measured as Total AR
* Incoming Students
* Retention & Academic Compliance

* No order of importance implied. Current focus on improving financial compliance without detriment to other ultimate outcomes.

of a signed "student financial agreement" for each student became one of Enrollment's indicators of success. This was not considered a change (or tweak) to the process, but rather a monitor to see if the process was functioning as intended.

Each function represented on the PRT proposed a set of indicators to define and monitor its own process outputs. Just as with the enrollment example, representatives established these indicators based on the functional outputs and issues identified in the process clarification meeting. Once there was agreement within the PRT on the total set of indicators, or "alignment" of indicators, each department began tracking itself against these indicators and presenting the data in weekly PRT meetings.

Step 4. Hold Frequent Process Review Team (PRT) Meetings

OBJECTIVE: Use the indicator data to identify bottlenecks.

Remember that before a process can be systemically improved, its current capability must be understood. At this stage, the PRT was simply gauging how capable each function was (with the existing resources) of producing what was necessary to support overall success. Figure 3.4 shows data from Enrollment's new indicator of a signed student financial agreement from each student. In this case, performance improved from zero to about 80 percent simply by putting the indicator in place. Figure 3.5 shows indicator data from a separate function: Financial Services. One responsibility of this function was to collect and validate financial aid paperwork so that it could be sent to the appropriate agency for qualification. It was important that this paperwork be 100 percent complete and accurate the first time; re-submitting the paperwork added critical aging time to the AR. As you can see from the graph, the goal was to submit 95 percent of the paperwork packets 100 percent complete the first time, but current performance ranged from 40–90 percent.

After monitoring the performance associated with each indicator for about six weeks, the PRT was ready to make decisions about where to start making changes. In today's fast-paced environments there often isn't time to discuss every decision until a cross-functional consensus is reached. At the same time, each function has unique knowledge of the process, and ignoring that knowledge would set up an organization for failure. The consultative approach to decision-making is designed to reach a compromise between the need for speed and the importance of well-informed decisions (Daniels, 1997). In this approach, a leader is empowered to be *the* decision maker, but this person is also expected to consult all appropriate stakeholders before making a decision. Instead of selecting a leader from Accounting, which would further reinforce the notion that this was an Accounting department problem, the PRT leader was selected from a function called Student Services. The PRT members agreed ahead of time that once a decision was made, everyone would commit to it even

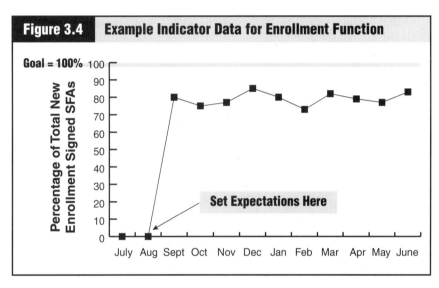

Figure 3.4 — **Example Indicator Data for Enrollment Function**

Figure 3.5 — **Example Indicator Data for Financial Services Function**

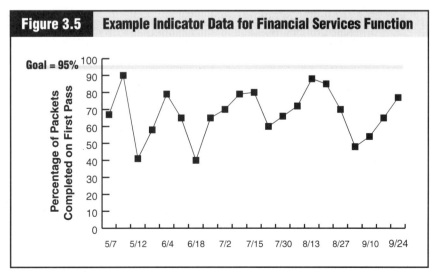

if consensus had not been achieved. The consultant attended the first several PRT meetings, and attended periodically after that in order to facilitate effective process management and consultative decision-making.

Step 5. Link to Individual/Small Group Performance Systems

OBJECTIVES: Engage performers in resolving the current bottleneck, and determine if ready to move on to the next bottleneck.

The indicators become the potential link to individual and small group level Performance Systems. To the extent that the individuals responsible for each indicator are tracking and monitoring their own performance, they are operating in the first two conditions of the individual PS (clear expectations and frequent self-monitored feedback). Ideally, indicators reported to the PRT should all be based on individual/small group Performance Systems. This individual/small group performance data is the most reliable data upon which to base decisions about process improvement. The question at this stage is: which aspect of process performance is most responsible for preventing overall process success?

Remember, based on the principles observed in the wafer fabrication plant, we don't want to change too many variables at the same time. Otherwise, even if overall process performance improves, we can't make the necessary correlation between a "tweak" and its result, and the overall change will not be sustained. We want to identify the biggest bottleneck in the process and address it so that it will be unlikely to return. One of the big bottlenecks discovered early on in this case was the failure to turn in 100 percent complete and accurate paperwork packets the first time (as evidenced by the data in figure 3.5).

At first it was a little puzzling that packet completeness performance hadn't taken care of itself (as enrollment performance had) once the indicator was being tracked and the contributors to this output were seemingly in a PS. The PRT determined, however, that although these performers were generating self-feedback about their performance, they did not have clear expectations aligned with overall process success. The performers did not report to the department responsible for financial aid compliance; they reported instead to the managers of each individual campus. The campus managers were rewarded (formally

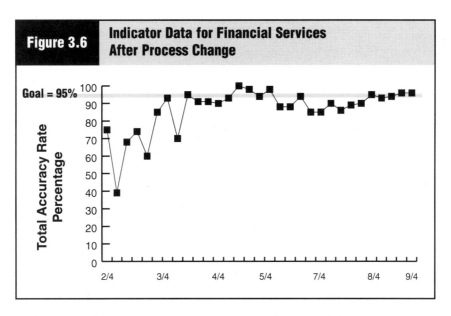

Figure 3.6 | **Indicator Data for Financial Services After Process Change**

and informally) primarily for customer satisfaction. If the students from a certain campus began calling into senior university management with complaints, it was the campus manager who heard about it. The performers responsible for the paperwork packets were aware that packet completeness was a goal (due to frequent e-mails from the manager of "some other department"), but they also knew that one way to upset students was to continue "hassling" them about their paperwork. When students were unhappy they complained, and this was the easiest way to get on the wrong side of the campus manager. For the sake of the overall process, the performers needed to report directly to the manager who was responsible for financial aid compliance. Once this transition was made, the performance expectations became clear, and the performance against the packet completeness indicator rose to around 90 percent, where it has mostly remained (see figure 3.6).

Many PRT members were concerned that with this change, even if the completeness rate improved, customer service would get worse. So while the entire Financial Services team was focusing on packet completeness, a sub-team was tasked to look at how to measure and improve customer service. As a result, the group reorganized itself (with PRT support) to include a call center, so that constant feedback on customer service would be available.

Step 6. Document Results

OBJECTIVE: Use performance data to show the impact of the PS approach.

In addition to the indicator measurements, the PRT would periodically review overall process performance, especially total AR. When Raven University began the PS intervention, total AR and the percentage of AR over 90 days old continued to rise for a couple months. But as bottlenecks were removed, AR peaked and began a slow descent. AR naturally increases as enrollment increases, and enrollment was rising steadily throughout the period depicted in the graph. The point is that rather than continuing to trend upwards, disproportionate to enrollment, AR came back into proportion with current enrollment. (The appropriate proportion of AR to enrollment was determined using a separate measure called "days of sales outstanding.") After the PRT had been in existence for a little over one year, the AR level was back down to the level appropriate to current enrollment, and equally important, the AR trend has stayed relatively stable at the appropriate level. It was now time for the PRT to look at the possibility of improving any other ultimate success measures (enrollment growth or educational quality) while maintaining AR at normal levels.

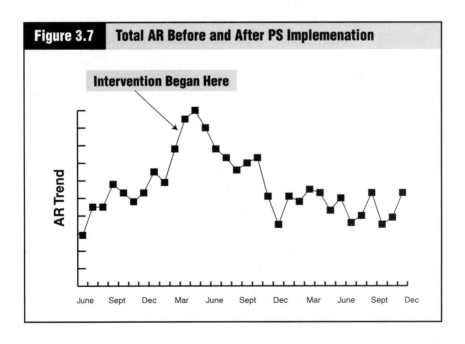

| Figure 3.7 | Total AR Before and After PS Implemenation |

Figure 3.7 shows the changes to the end result measures just described.

Since the client owns this data, there's no need to convince them of the value of the intervention; they will see it for themselves and be more likely to promote expansion of the PS. In addition to this quantifiable data, the most obvious long-term change at Raven University is the ongoing presence of the PRT. Having this cross-functional body permanently in place has increased communication and collaboration both at the process level and the management staff level. A more subtle change is how this organization, which had been very reactive, is learning to collect data and discuss the consequences of process changes *before* they are implemented. In the early stages of the intervention, the PRT constantly had to be reminded not to jump to problem solving too soon. Now they usually catch themselves and self-correct. As a result, there are fewer changes occurring, but those changes tend to yield sustainable results. As of this writing, the university is continuing to apply Performance Systems throughout the organization.

Step 7. Link to Next Level Up in the Organization

OBJECTIVE: Expand the scope of the PS in the organization.

Once an organization has learned to manage a core process as a PS, the best way to ensure that it continues to do so is to take the concept of the PS up one more level to support management of the whole organization. Chapter 5 will use a separate case to describe this concept and how it is accomplished. But as mentioned at the outset of this chapter, cross-functional work takes the form of either processes or projects. Although there are several parallels between applying this approach on processes and projects, the differences make it worthwhile to provide a project-oriented example of the cross-functional Performance System. That will be the focus of chapter 4.

Question & Answer

1. How and where is it determined whether to approach the business problem with a process- or project-oriented approach?

During the sponsor meeting it should become apparent whether the current business challenge is around ongoing work (a process) or work with a specific and defined endpoint (project). Usually it is pretty obvious which way to go, but occasionally framing the work as process or project is a judgment call. For example, one organization originally asked for help with a specific type of information technology project. As an organization, they were implementing many of these types of projects at one time. But it turned out that these projects were part of a larger cross-functional process for supporting client databases. In that case, although the request was for help with projects, it made more sense to address the larger process.

2. Wasn't there resistance from the large group to turn things over to the smaller process review team after the process clarification meeting?

In this case, there was not. This may be due to the fact that the process review team didn't actually meet for three months after the process clarification meeting. Senior management was intent on responding to certain issues that were beyond the control of the PRT before turning things over to them. With that in mind, they held weekly meetings, led by the senior campus manager, to address those issues. During the three months of meetings, they realized that the campus manager was committed to this process, and that resolving the issues would take cross-functional cooperation. By the time senior management turned the reins over to the process review team, people understood that this was not just going to be another quick fix effort, and there was relatively little resistance at any level in the organization. There was also a concerted effort to

Question & Answer

communicate to everyone how and why the process review team was selected, and what their charter would be.

3. How do you ensure that the process review team members pick the right indicators?

The consultant should provide some general guidance and examples to the PRT members before they work on their indicators. Most importantly, they need to focus on the key process outputs and top issues identified in the process clarification meeting. Some PRT members will be better at drafting indicators than others. However, during the alignment step, each PRT member will have input into each other's indicators. The right indicators will tell the PRT members if each functional area is achieving its process output goals. From a coaching standpoint, a consultant needs to find the balance between beginning with technically sound performance measures and letting the team learn what works best. Inevitably, the team will learn and indicators will be fine-tuned over time. In general, it is more important that the PRT members feel ownership for their indicators than to have everything documented the way the consultant would do it.

4. If you begin at the process level, how do you ensure each functional team is already operating in individual/ small group performance systems?

When the functional representatives of the PRT are developing indicators, they should be encouraged to base those indicators on self-tracked performance data. But not all of them will follow this advice; they may already have an automated tracking system in place that makes it relatively easy to collect and assemble indicator data. These "management information systems," designed to inform management about what is going on in the work environment, are often not very reliable sources of data (see figure 1.1). However, they will suffice to get the PRT up and running. As the PRT begins examining the data and identifying issues, there will be opportunities to educate the group on the value of self-tracking and to introduce contributors to individual/small group performance systems.

5. How did you know that the people processing the financial aid packets didn't just need more/better training on how to process packets?

There had been a number of informal training sessions held with the performers to make sure they understood the most common reasons packets were not done right the first time. These sessions may have had some impact, but clearly, too many packets still had errors. One of the lessons learned by the PRT was that performance problems are not always solved by training or retraining the performers. Throughout the course of the intervention, the PRT dealt with all the various factors that impact performance (knowledge and skills, proper tools, feedback, inappropriate consequences, unclear expectations, capability, or motivation, as per Gilbert, Mager and Pipe, Rummler, and others). This is where Performance Systems meet the more conventional performance analysis approach, but it's important to note that the role of the consultant was to coach the PRT and various functional sub-teams through performance analysis rather than do it for them.

6. Why is a distinction made between "indicator" and the measure "Total AR"?

I find it valuable to distinguish between what I call "end result" measures and "indicators." While indicators are designed to predict if we are likely to achieve desired end results, end result measures tell us if in fact they were met. A recent article about the golfer Tiger Woods may help clarify this distinction.

As described in the August 14, 2000 issue of *Time Magazine*, after Tiger Woods won the Master's in 1998, he decided that although he was winning, his swing could be improved. Tiger's end result measure of success is tournaments won (especially the major tournaments), but he knew that if he was going to get even better he would have to forgo some wins and just work on his swing. So Tiger stopped focusing on the end result measure (winning tournaments) in 1999 and instead focused on the indicators of a quality golf swing: the position of his hands, where the ball was landing, and the feel of his swing. Although Tiger was winning fewer tournaments, his indicators told him he was moving toward his goal. In the 2000 season, Tiger's work paid off as measured by tournament wins and dollars earned (he became the second golfer ever to win three of the four major tournaments in one year and collected twice as much in winnings as any other golfer on the tour).

Accordingly, when improving the performance of a cross-functional process, it is important to stop responding to every blip in the end result measure and focus on identifying and improving the key indicators. When this is done as described in this chapter, the end results will take care of themselves.

7. How can you be sure that this improvement was due entirely or even primarily to implementing the process-oriented PS?

I do not believe it should be the goal of performance consultants to prove beyond doubt that specific improvements can be attributed to specific interventions. The types of experimental controls necessary to provide such evidence are usually not feasible in a business environment. More importantly, I've never met a client that considered such evidence necessary. When a series of indicator improvements are followed by the desired end result improvement, there's not much point in arguing over what caused what. The most important indicator of whether a Performance System is really effective is if the improvements persist over time. Consistent with earlier discussions in this book, the goal of this approach is not just episodic improvements but systemic sustainable improvements. The total AR graph clearly shows that for whatever reason, performance stabilized at the post-intervention level.

CHAPTER 4

STAYING ON TRACK: SYSTEMS FOR PROJECT MANAGEMENT

Why Projects Fail

ALTHOUGH THERE ARE VARIATIONS ON THE THEME of project management, most of what is taught today is not much different than what has been taught for the last fifty years. Breaking work down into smaller and smaller chunks (phases, milestones, tasks, subtasks, etc.), estimating the time to complete each chunk, defining the resources that will contribute to each chunk, and periodically checking the status on work—these are the basics that are addressed in just about every project management book or class. This would be fine if the nature of projects and the environment they occur in also had not changed, but this is not the case. The relationship between management and performer has changed significantly, global markets have created much more intense competition, and we've moved from the industrial age to the information age, just to name a few substantial changes.

In industry today, time is generally believed to be *more* valuable than money, and yet it is typical for a company's critical projects to take 30-50 percent longer than planned. Much of this schedule slippage is a function of rework. As project teams face pressure to go faster and faster, they take shortcuts and make errors which come back and impact the schedule toward the end of projects. Conventional project management techniques not only fail to prevent these unhappy circumstances, but often exacerbate them. I refer to this dynamic as the project management vicious cycle. (It is also one of those predictable sets of symptoms and causes that performance consultants can apply to increase their credibility with potential clients.) Unless some changes are made to the way projects are managed (and the way project management is taught), it seems unlikely that typical projects will reliably achieve their goals anytime soon.

The project-oriented PS has been applied to some of the most complex projects in some of today's most pressure-packed environments. When it is applied effectively, projects reliably perform to within plus or minus 10 percent of their schedules with improved quality and significantly less performer overtime. **The key is to get most of the project team performing in the three PS conditions most of the time.** Although the terminology is a little different from process implementations, a project-oriented PS contains the same major components. For example, instead of a process clarification meeting, project implementations involve a team planning meeting. Instead of developing and aligning indicators, the project implementation involves defining a deliverables-based plan. And in both cases, actual performance needs to be monitored against planned performance, and the right people need to review that data and make appropriate adjustments in a timely fashion. The steps are similar because the intentions are similar: get every contributor to the project operating with clear expectations, frequent self-monitored feedback and the belief that when issues are raised the focus will be on resolving them.

I describe the application of the project-oriented PS in detail in my book: *No Surprises Project Management* (1999). The purpose of this chapter is to demonstrate the parallels that exist between project- and process-oriented implementations. Again, implementation follows a step-by-step sequence as shown in figure 4.1, and a brief case walks you through those steps.

Figure 4.1	**Project-Oriented Performance System Implementation Flowchart**

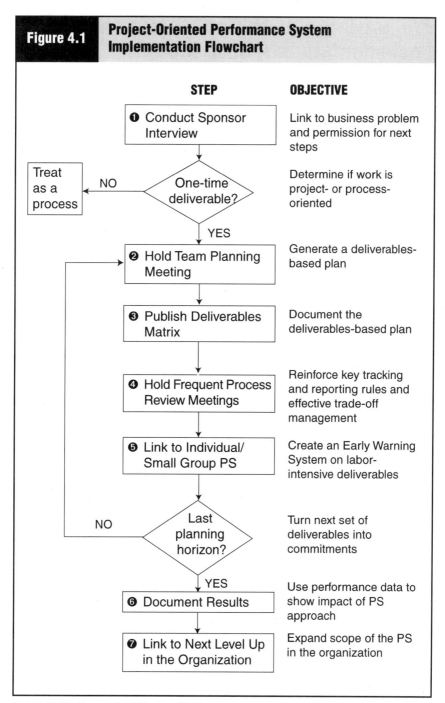

STEP	OBJECTIVE
❶ Conduct Sponsor Interview	Link to business problem and permission for next steps
One-time deliverable? — NO → Treat as a process	Determine if work is project- or process-oriented
❷ Hold Team Planning Meeting	Generate a deliverables-based plan
❸ Publish Deliverables Matrix	Document the deliverables-based plan
❹ Hold Frequent Process Review Meetings	Reinforce key tracking and reporting rules and effective trade-off management
❺ Link to Individual/ Small Group PS	Create an Early Warning System on labor-intensive deliverables
Last planning horizon?	Turn next set of deliverables into commitments
❻ Document Results	Use performance data to show impact of PS approach
❼ Link to Next Level Up in the Organization	Expand scope of the PS in the organization

Project-Oriented Performance System Implementation: A Case Study

In 1997, it was clear that television and computer technologies were on a collision course. What was not clear was if the television would swallow the computer, or the computer would swallow the television. So although no one was quite sure what the consumer wanted, hi-tech companies were clamoring to hit on the right combination and bring the first high-demand hybrid TV/computer to market.

One product development team had heard about the project-oriented PS and asked for assistance in applying it to their project. Their charter was to create a product that would sit on top of the TV and, roughly speaking, turn the TV into a computer. Because the market was not well understood, the marketing phase of the project would be more involved than usual. At the same time, because of the race to be first, it also had to be as swift as possible. I had written about the peril of succumbing to market pressure in high tech environments before, and those stories were what sold the team on Performance Systems.

Step 1. Conduct Sponsor Interview

OBJECTIVES: Link to the business problem and get permission for next steps. Determine if work is project- or process-oriented.

In this case, the sponsor meeting consisted mostly of answering questions the sponsor had after hearing about Performance Systems. The business problem was to determine the appropriate nature of this product and develop it in a timely fashion. The sponsor was convinced after asking his questions that the PS could help them achieve their goal. In this case, it was clear the project was not part of a larger process. The consultant "kicked off" the PS intervention with a team planning meeting.

Step 2. Hold Team Planning Meeting

OBJECTIVE: Generate a deliverables-based plan.

In order to achieve clear expectations for each project contributor, there first needs to be a clear high-level project plan that has substantial input from all project contributors. After some pre-work was done with upper management to establish the desired high-level project priorities (business goals, schedule, quality and cost considerations), the entire team met for a day and a half to create the high-level plan. As with the Process Clarification Meeting, the role of the consultant is to coach management on setting up the meeting and then facilitate the meeting according to the objectives and agenda. Figure 4.2 shows this meeting's agenda. The meeting is structured to get everyone's input into the basic sequence of events, the key hand-offs from one functional area to another (e.g., from Marketing to Design, from Design to Test, etc.) and very importantly, clear definitions of the required quality of those hand-offs. The key to this clarity is to ensure that the team develops the plan in terms of deliverables (a.k.a., accomplishments, outcomes) rather than tasks and activities. So, for example, instead of describing the marketing phase as "making the business case," "generating potential customers," and "identifying critical product features," the team needs to agree on the specific outcomes from these tasks and how the quality of those outcomes will be judged. The marketing phase would better be described as "first go/no go decisions," "design wins," and "product requirements document." Once the plan had been drafted in terms of deliverables, the team determined who would contribute to each specific deliverable, who would be the single "owner" for each deliverable, and who would be the designated "users" of each deliverable.

One practice that can cause project goals to get fuzzy is asking people to put dates on work that they won't be starting for weeks or months. It is common for management to ask for *estimates* which over time become misconstrued as *commitments* from the team. The solution to this problem is to have the team put dates only on those deliverables they are comfortable committing to at the current time. In this case, by the end of the team planning meeting, the team was able to commit to most of the deliverables in the marketing phase, but only a few deliverables from the design phase. This meant that the team needed to meet periodically throughout the project to apply dates further into the schedule. The part of the schedule that the team is comfortable applying dates to at any one time is called the current "planning horizon."

Figure 4.2	**Two-Day Agenda for a Team Planning Meeting**		
DAY 1			
ITEM	**ACTIVITY**	**OUTCOME**	**EST. TIME**
1	Sponsor Presentation	Define customer, ultimate project deliverable and high level success criteria.	10 min.
2	Housekeeping Warm-Up Activity Meeting Agenda/Roles Ground Rules	Clear expectations for this meeting.	50 min.
3	Define Customer Deliverables	3-7 tangible things we will deliver to the customer(s).	60 min.
4	Define Internal Deliverables	8-12 major things that must be produced along the way to deliver each customer deliverable.	90 min.
5	Validate the Deliverables Map	Sequence of events: who will deliver what to whom.	60 min.
Day 2			
6	Walk Through the Map	Identify holes and disconnects. Identify the rough critical path.	60 min.
7	Define Quality Requirements for Internal Deliverables	Criteria for each internal deliverable.	120 min.
8	Make First Horizon Commitments	When teams can commit to deliver specific early deliverables.	45 min.
9	Wrap Up/Next Steps	Issues turned into actions and expectations about what the team will do with meeting outcomes.	30 min.

© 2001 The Center for Effective Performance, Inc.

Step 3. Publish Deliverables Matrix

OBJECTIVE: Document the deliverables-based plan.

The desired outcome of the team planning meeting is to initiate a dialogue—to get the right people talking about the right things. The desired result of this is clear documentation of the high-level project plan. Figure 4.3 shows a portion of the team's "deliverables matrix." The form of this document is negotiable, but all of the content shown in the column heads is critical. The deliverables matrix becomes the source for both clear expectations and frequent feedback at the cross-functional level of the project. In regards to clear expectations, it specifies who will deliver what to whom when, and to what quality requirements. To establish frequent feedback, the deliverables matrix is used to structure regular progress review meetings.

Figure 4.3	Partial Deliverables Matrix

Deliverables	Owner	User(s)	Quality Req's	Commit Date	Done?
Project Plan	Jake	Debra, Lee Bill, Jenifer	Y	WW10	
Architecture Doc.	Debra	Bill, Jenifer	Y	WW13	
Product Spec.	Debra	Bill, Jenifer	Y	WW15	
Demand Schedule	Lee	Jake	Y	WW15	
1st Prototype	Bill	Jenifer	N	WW18	
Test Plan	Jenifer	Bill	Y	WW17	

Note: WW= Workweek

Step 4. Hold Frequent Progress Review Meetings

OBJECTIVE: Reinforce key tracking and reporting rules and effective trade-off management.

Progress reviews were structured so that most of the time was spent anticipating and preventing slips (schedule, quality, and/or cost). Review meant verifying that any scheduled deliverables were in fact done. This was almost cursory, because for several weeks leading up to any deliverable due date, the owners of each deliverable were reporting on current progress and identifying any issues that might create a slip if not addressed. At this stage, the role of the consultant is to help the team leader structure the meetings and then observe and coach periodically on decision-making and key ground rules. Most of the decision-making in these meetings was about how to address *potential* issues, rather than how to recover from crises, which is the focus of much of the discussion in conventional project reviews.

One meeting ground rule must be followed by all team members: each owner is obligated to raise any issue that might prevent him or her from meeting his or her commit date as soon as that issue becomes apparent (provide early warning). The flip side of this rule is that the rest of the team must respond to each identified issue supportively (don't kill the messenger). In other words, raising issues ahead of time leads to problem solving and an open discussion of trade-offs, rather than chastisement or finger pointing. When this ground rule is followed, team members are taking responsibility for the overall project goals, instead of defending their own functional territories to avoid blame.

Step 5. Link to Individual/Small Group Performance System

OBJECTIVES: Create an Early Warning System on labor-intensive deliverables, and turn next set of deliverables into commitments.

In order for each deliverable owner to be sure about the current status of his or her deliverables, he or she needs to have accurate performance data from team members for the weekly progress review. Deliverable owners (usually designated team leaders who own and report on deliverables for a specific functional team) should have short weekly meetings with their teams of individual contributors before they attend the project level progress review. These "sub-team" meetings are structured around an individual/ small group performance system.

For any labor-intensive deliverables, owners should delineate clear expectations for each individual contributor. A labor-intensive deliverable is one that will require multiple contributors multiple weeks to complete. For example, one such deliverable in the marketing phase of this project was "design wins" for the product. A design win is when a customer company agrees to buy the product, incorporate it into their own product offerings, or possibly design it into their own product. If the product cannot attract enough design wins, it is a waste of time to design and produce it. Several marketing personnel were contributing to the design wins deliverable, and the team needed a way to monitor their progress reliably. To accomplish this, just before the weekly progress review, the deliverable owner would meet with the marketing team and ask each team member three questions:

1. How did you perform against your goal this week (in terms of new design wins)?

2. What is your goal for new design wins for next week?

3. Are their any issues that are likely to prevent us from achieving our deliverable goal?

This marketing sub-team is just one example of teams and individuals using small-scale performance systems to determine if they were on track to meet their key deliverable commitments. Not every deliverable on the matrix needs to be managed with its own performance system, but labor-intensive deliverables do. Otherwise, the risk is too great that sub-teams will not discover they are behind until it is too late to do anything about it. On a project, any individual or group that has committed to provide deliverables needs to ensure on-time delivery. The individual and small group PS is a tool to help them do so.

The project-level progress review meeting and the sub-team level meetings use a similar agenda and follow the same basic ground rule to ensure that accurate performance data is reported throughout the project and that each team member is operating in the three PS conditions. Both of these meetings are driven by the deliverables matrix, which is the outcome of the team planning meeting. Towards the end of each planning horizon, another team planning meeting is conducted to put more dates on the deliverables matrix. As shown in figure 4.1, each new planning horizon requires cycling back through the key planning and tracking steps. When this approach is working well (and it always will if the agendas and ground rules are followed), teams meet their deliverable commit dates consistently and develop confidence in their planning abilities. As people develop the confidence to commit further out into the future, the planning horizons get longer and schedules get more aggressive. But the aggressive scheduling is coming from the team members themselves, and they are more committed to succeed than ever.

Step 6. Document Results

OBJECTIVE: Use performance data to show the impact of the PS approach.

One tool used to track project performance was the performance against commitment (PAC) chart (see figure 4.4). The PAC chart is a summary indicator of whether the team is likely to meet its committed end date. As long as the bars are meeting or are very close to meeting the goal line (dots), the team is in good shape. The principle here is that the only reliable predictor of future performance is past performance. Teams that have been meeting their commitments consistently for the first three months of a project are very likely to do so for the next three months, because they are obviously serious about their commitments and have no doubt made good trade-off decisions. Figure 4.4 shows this team's performance against commitment for the first eleven weeks of the project.

Interestingly enough, in this case, the design wins indicated a few

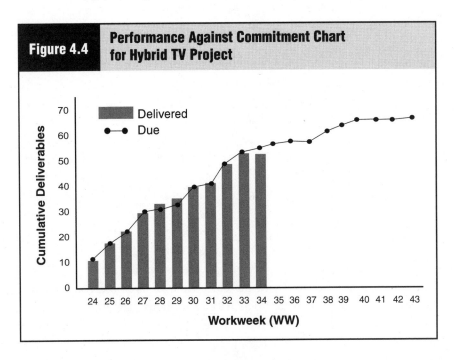

Figure 4.4 — **Performance Against Commitment Chart for Hybrid TV Project**

months into the project that customers were not very interested in this product in this particular configuration, and the project was cancelled. Though some might argue that this is a poor example because it was cancelled, the sponsor considered it a project management success. New product ideas have, at most, a 20 percent chance of success, and yet many new product teams continue investing resources in the wrong ideas for months and even years. This team had confidence in the data it was generating, and after seeing disappointing design win numbers for several weeks in a row, they (and their sponsors) concluded that this was the wrong product or the wrong time. The team moved on to more promising projects and, courtesy of the PAC chart, they did so with their heads held high, knowing that they had performed well against their plans.

Step 7. Link to Next Level Up in the Organization

OBJECTIVE: Expand the scope of the PS in the organization.

The descriptions of both the process example in chapter 3 and this project example have been simplified for brevity, but the results are real. In both cases, a participative meeting was used to plan successful performance and measures were put in place to quantify and compare actual performance to the plan. In both cases, the individuals and functional groups were accustomed to some form of planning and tracking, but for fairly predictable reasons, it was not resulting in reliable or successful performance. However, with some coaching on effective performance systems, these teams learned to manage themselves towards success. And they will be able to put these same structures and principles into practice on any other project or process they choose.

Most product development organizations like the one in this case are designing many products simultaneously, just as construction companies work on many structures at the same time. The only way to ensure that all the important projects in the organization are managed effectively is to implement a PS in the next level up in the organization: the people who manage project managers (and their bosses). Chapter 5 will provide another unique case which addresses taking the PS to the organization-wide level.

Question & Answer

1. How can you possibly do effective project planning (or have any type of effective meeting for that matter) with 50 people in the room?

At least a quarter of the cross-functional meetings I have held have involved 50–100 participants. First of all, it is very important that a team planning meeting be inclusive rather than exclusive. (The same is true for the process clarification meeting in a process-oriented PS.) If the goal is for the people doing the work to help manage the work, then they need to be included in establishing the PS, especially up front. When people are given an opportunity to participate in the early stages, they are much more likely to empower others to make management decisions for them later.

The same basic meeting structures and techniques can be used for both process clarification meetings (process-oriented) and team planning meetings (project-oriented). These structures and instructions for implementing them are provided in detail in my book *No Surprises Project Management* (1999). The basic idea is to get the group focused on one meeting agenda item at a time, have a way for each individual to share his or her assumptions and test the assumptions of others, and then move towards a shared decision for that agenda item. For groups larger than about 100 people, multiple meetings may need to be held, just because of logistical issues (e.g., room size and acoustics).

2. What do the quality requirements for each specific deliverable look like?

The owner and users for each deliverable need to talk about quality before work begins on any specific deliverable. The basic aim of the conversation should be agreement on how to know when the deliverable is done, and done well. I usually recommend that any documented requirements be kept and monitored by the owner and users themselves (rather than being used as a management tool to oversee the team members). The deliverables matrix has a column to prompt the project manager to ask deliverable owners if they've had this conversation with the users. Also, when a deliverable is declared "done," the project manager is well-advised to ask the users if they received what was agreed to. In regards to formatting the requirements, sometimes owners and users just brainstorm lists of what the deliverable "is" and "is not" supposed to be. In other cases, teams are more specific about distinguishing between the required content of a deliverable, the required quality of the deliverable and some simple measures of success.

3. **If the team only puts dates on the schedule for the current project horizon, how do the customers of the project know when they can expect the project outcomes?**

Paradoxically, the urgent need for project end dates is the catalyst of the downward spiral I call the project management vicious cycle. But there is an easy solution to this problem. Until a given project team has been operating in a performance system for a while, their estimates of project end dates are typically no better, and many times worse, than an estimate created by a few high-level managers and contributors. In other words, there is usually an end date in mind before a large project gets funded, and that date is as good as any estimate the team will generate at the beginning of the project. (Long-term estimates are notoriously inaccurate, for a variety of reasons.) Brooks (1975), in one of the more popular project management books, referred to this initial estimate as the "external schedule goal" because it is the date management and marketing should use to communicate to external partners and customers until they establish an internal schedule goal.

Question & Answer

4. You keep referring to predictable patterns of performance, but how can a novice at this approach recognize and articulate all these different patterns?

It may sound like a variety of different patterns, but really it is all the same one. We've already seen the project management vicious cycle in action at the individual/small group level in chapter 2 and in the process-oriented example in chapter 3. In chapter 2, the pattern was described as responding to jobs behind schedule rather than preventing jobs from falling behind. In chapter 3, the pattern was described as accounts receivables pushing out in time because key components of the existing process were not being followed. When an organization focuses on reacting to problems rather than preventing them, they will:

a) perform poorly on time-sensitive measures (e.g., schedule);

b) pass off sub-standard quality (in order to hurry and try to meet schedules);

c) experience "finger-pointing" between functional areas, because sub-standard quality is being passed from one function to the next;

d) produce little or inaccurate performance data rather than risk being blamed for performance issues;

e) base important resource management decisions on something other than accurate performance data (because it is not available);

f) never set goals with structured input from the performers themselves, which is how this whole cycle gets started (remember personal commitment, the pearl in the onion).

Question & Answer

5. Since sales is a transactional process, how would a marketing team member be able to predict the number of design wins for a specific week?

Getting a design win involves several distinct tasks: identifying prospects, getting in to make a presentation, and closing the sale. Marketing and sales people are taught that in order to achieve a certain number of sales, you have to have a proportionate number of sales presentations, since only a percentage of presentations will lead to sales. And likewise, in order to ensure a certain number of presentations, you will need maybe two to five times that many prospects. In order to know whether they were on track to hit their design win goal, marketing needed to hit weekly prospect and presentation goals. If they fell behind these goals, they were obligated to inform the team. But to the extent they stayed on or ahead of goals, they could assume that the deliverable commitment was safe.

6. You've referenced two new project planning and tracking tools (deliverables matrix and PAC chart), but what about the standard Gantt-type chart that is produced by the typical project management software program?

My recommendation to project teams is that they use the two new tools instead of the conventional project schedule (Gantt chart). I recommend this because Gantt charts are typically task-based rather than deliverables-based, and they put too much emphasis on estimates at the expense of commit dates. There is sometimes resistance to this advice because project managers and team leaders want to be able to adjust the schedule based on slips as they occur. Project management software usually makes it easy to "calculate" the impact of a schedule change to the rest of the schedule. However, teams that use the project-oriented PS and associated tools don't need this feature much, because they prevent slips

78 ──────────────────────────────────── MAKING AN **IMPACT**

Question & Answer

instead of responding to them. Some teams choose to use both sets of tools until they become comfortable with the PS approach.

7. **Decision-making in the project-level progress reviews and sub-team meetings seems to be crucial to success. Is it assumed that teams are good at decision-making?**

No. A key role of the consultant is to facilitate effective decision-making when these meetings are just beginning. These decision-making principles apply at all levels in the organization.

Whenever the team's performance data indicates that they may not achieve their plan, a decision needs to be made. The team should already have agreed to an ongoing decision-making process. As mentioned in chapter 3, I recommend consultative decision-making, where the team empowers the leader to make decisions after he or she has heard all interested parties. Decisions typically should follow a sound problem solving process. For example:

- State the issue or problem (difference between desired and expected result).

- Validate the problem (review performance data and other relevant data).

- Discuss alternatives (move towards recommendations).

- Leader considers all recommendations and makes a decision.

- Leader clearly states and explains decision.

- Follow up on resulting action plan (verify actions implemented and evaluate results, revisit if appropriate).

CHAPTER 5

A VIEW FROM THE TOP: ORGANIZATION-WIDE SYSTEMS

Smart Boundaries

WE'VE BECOME ACCUSTOMED TO HEARING that organizations that are too hierarchical and bureaucratic cannot cope in today's fast-paced, complex, and competitive environments. Hierarchy and bureaucracy have not always been looked down upon by organizational theorists; both actually evolved as solutions to the problems of increasing scale and complexity in organizations (Beniger, 1986; Pinchot and Pinchot, 1993). Large-scale organizations probably would not exist without them. The question is not so much how to do away with hierarchy and bureaucracy as how to adapt them to work in today's environment.

Today's most effective large organizations are still hierarchically and functionally structured, but they work effectively across these artificial boundaries. More precisely, they've learned to recognize boundaries when doing so makes sense (e.g., to simplify administration and achieve uniform treatment of employees), and ignore boundaries where they unnecessarily obstruct achieving desired results. No organization does this flawlessly, but the best organizations do a better job than others. Accomplishing this requires implementing a PS not only at the individual/ small group and cross-functional levels of the organization, but also at the top, where organization-wide goals are set and monitored. The term "organization-wide" as the third level of PS implementation really refers to the level where goals for the organization as a whole are set, whatever that may be specifically in your organization. So in an organization-wide Performance System, the senior management team is continuously clarifying expectations, reviewing progress against those expectations, and deciding, given the latest information, on the best way to utilize the organization's overall resources.

In order to increase the range of real examples in this book, we will move to a new case describing a PS implementation at the senior staff level. Bill Daniels agreed to revisit a success story that he originally documented in 1997, just as one of his clients was getting a PS established at the senior management level and beginning to let it migrate downward. The case will be structured around the last of the four flowcharts for implementation: the seven sequential steps to an organization-wide PS implementation (see figure 5.1). For more background on this case and Daniel's more detailed treatment of this approach, see his book, *Change-ABLE Organization: Key Management Practices for Speed and Flexibility* (1997).

Organization-Wide Performance System Implementation: A Case Study

Step 1. Conduct Sponsor Interview

OBJECTIVES: Link to the business problem and get permission for next steps.

In 1993, a relatively small semiconductor equipment producer began shaking up its leadership team. The company hoped to improve its financial performance by taking advantage of an emerging business opportunity. The market for Etec Systems, Inc.'s core products, mask pattern generation equipment, had been basically flat for the previous ten years. But new levels of miniaturization in the semiconductor industry were going to require a breakthrough in mask pattern technology. Etec hoped to capitalize on

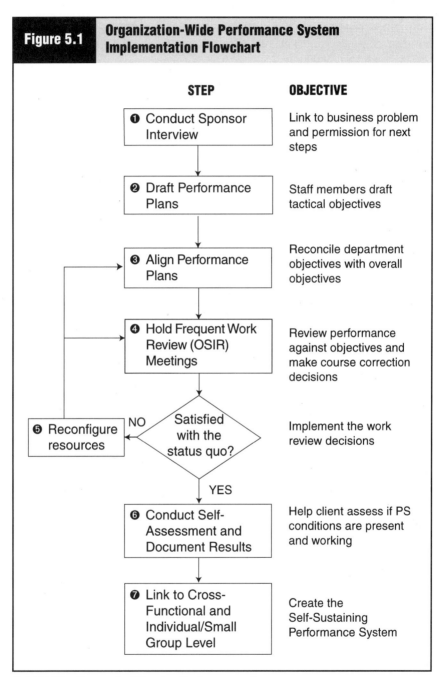

| Figure 5.1 | Organization-Wide Performance System Implementation Flowchart |

STEP   **OBJECTIVE**

❶ Conduct Sponsor Interview — Link to business problem and permission for next steps

❷ Draft Performance Plans — Staff members draft tactical objectives

❸ Align Performance Plans — Reconcile department objectives with overall objectives

❹ Hold Frequent Work Review (OSIR) Meetings — Review performance against objectives and make course correction decisions

Satisfied with the status quo? — NO

❺ Reconfigure resources — Implement the work review decisions

YES

❻ Conduct Self-Assessment and Document Results — Help client assess if PS conditions are present and working

❼ Link to Cross-Functional and Individual/Small Group Level — Create the Self-Sustaining Performance System

© 2001 The Center for Effective Performance, Inc.

this. But they were struggling internally; Etec had recently merged with another company and key technical members of each former company were at odds over the best solution. The company seemed well-positioned to expand its market, but it would have to decide how to focus its resources in order to get a new product to market quickly. By the time Etec considered getting help with its management systems, the leadership team had been restructured. The new team was tentative in its performance, and conflicts within the organization were still simmering.

After discussions with the new CEO and director of HR, and some further data collection, the performance consultant proposed that a good start would be to re-establish an effective performance feedback loop. Specifically, the consultant advocated improving the way the organization's goals were set, and ensuring they were monitored and supported through regular staff meetings. He proposed implementing a PS beginning at the top, the senior staff level, and then working down through the organization.

For several months, the sponsors were tentative about the breadth and ambiguity of the proposed solution. They had been hoping to get help solving some of the tangible and urgent problems in the organization (what I described in chapter 1 as having their problems solved for them). The concept of consulting on the management "process," rather than just solving the problems at hand, was testing their assumptions about the role of a consultant. It was actually the Sales department that finally got the ball rolling, when they asked the consultant to help design and facilitate a global sales meeting. The sales team ended up using that meeting to get aligned around a common set of goals and plans. Weeks later, tangible results began to appear, and the CEO gave the green light to implement the PS with his staff.

Step 2. Draft Performance Plans

OBJECTIVE: Staff members draft tactical objectives.

Performance plans are a manager's version of clear expectations. The consultant explained to the CEO and his staff that every manager in the organization needed to be able to articulate planned deliverables and priorities for the use of all the resources he or she managed and influenced—*and articulate it in less than three minutes.* In other words, they needed to clarify what each department intended to accomplish during the next nine

Figure 5.2	**Performance Plan for Overall Organization**

CEO (Overall Organization) Performance Plan

OBJECTIVES		PRIORITY	KEY PARTNERS
1. Gross Margin	47%	35%	
Operating Income	17%		
2. Orders: systems orders	> $100MM	35%	
support orders	> $ 35MM		
new products	> $ 12MM		
3. Expenses: Marketing & sales at < 6% of revenues		15%	
4. Headcount 215		15%	

Figure 5.3	**Performance Plan for the Sales Department**

VP Sales Performance Plan

SUPPORTS CEO OBJECTIVE #	OBJECTIVES	PRIORITY	KEY PARTNERS
2	1. Customer Satisfaction: Annual survey rating of >4	35%	VP Cust. Support.
1	2. Market Share ($)>70% worldwide	25%	Int. GMs
4	3. Backlog Minimum 9 month product B/L at plan revenue levels	20%	VP Ops.
2	4. Start monthly reviews of Product Development Process by end of Q1	10%	VP Ops. VP Eng.
3,2	5. Build a world class marketing/sales support organization	15%	VP H.R.

to twelve months. Figure 5.2 shows an example performance plan in the suggested format which represents the organization's overall objectives. The whole senior staff is responsible for this set of objectives, but they are usually owned and tracked by the senior manager (in this case the CEO). Once these overall objectives were agreed upon, each department manager developed a set of objectives to support the overall ones. For example, figure 5.3 is the Sales department's Performance Plan.

Before they drafted their plans, staff members were given a few points of guidance:

- A clear plan must contain a limited number (usually between three and seven) of specific measurable objectives.

- Priorities should be set by spreading 100 percentage points among the objectives, rather than establishing an order of priority. When objectives have a priority order, the first priority is often viewed as the only one. Every objective is a commitment and a priority; the idea is to establish the relative amount of resources and focus that will be required on each objective.

- "Key Partners" should include those people or departments from whom you will need significant cooperation in order to meet your objectives.

Once each department head had drafted a performance plan for their department, the plans needed to be aligned.

Step 3. Align Performance Plans

OBJECTIVE: Reconcile department objectives with the overall objectives.

As at the cross-functional level, it's imperative that each staff member's plan align to the agreed-upon plans for the entire team—the organization as a whole. This required that the team agree on the overall plan and then work through each supporting plan. While each member of the staff presents his or her draft plans, the consultant uses pre-established ground rules and coaching skills to make sure that everyone is participating, concerns are aired, and effective decision-making drives discussion towards agreement.

It is typical for this alignment process to take several staff meetings; after all, this is where the staff determines what the focus will be and how success will be defined for the next nine to twelve months. In this case, it went rather rapidly and unexpectedly smoothly. Apparently the shake-up and establishment of a new leadership team had clarified the key business challenge: establish the next mask pattern technology, develop it, and create a market for it within about a year. The meeting processes in this step and the next are typically a departure from what the client has been doing, and so the consultant acted as coach on the meeting's agendas and process.

Step 4. Hold Frequent Work Review ("OSIR") Meetings

OBJECTIVE: Review performance against objectives and make course correction decisions.

The original consulting proposal was to re-establish the performance feedback loop. Just like the lower levels in the organization, this is about getting the right people speaking from performance data about how they are performing against established goals and how to intervene when plans are not being met. Also, like the lower levels, to be effective, performance feedback needs to be frequent and self-monitored. In this case, self-monitored means that staff members come to staff meetings prepared to report on their team's performance against established performance plans. Daniels (1997) recommends that these reports be produced in the OSIR format.

OSIR stands for: Objectives, Status, Issues and Recommendations. This format helps ground the discussion to established objectives (per the performance plans). As shown in figure 5.4, an OSIR report explains how current performance compares against the objective, and whether the owner of that objective believes action needs to be taken to ensure the objective will be met. "Issues" identify current or anticipated barriers to success. Whenever issues are perceived to exist, the perceiver is obligated to bring recommendations for how the issues might be resolved. Note in figure 5.4 that each OSIR report corresponds to one or more of the objectives from the performance plan (compare to figure 5.3).

Only cross-departmental issues (those that require the effort and cooperation of two or more departments to resolve) should be reported in OSIR meetings. In the OSIR example provided, the Sales manager had issues in regards to his performance plan objectives of customer satisfaction and market share. The project to develop the mask pattern equipment was moving into the documentation phase, but there was data to show that the prerequisite qualification and documentation deliverables had not been completed (in other words, Etec's development process was not being followed). Sales was concerned because both customer satisfaction ratings and market share had been impacted in the past due to shortcuts in the development process. The evidence that this is a cross-departmental issue lies in the

Figure 5.4	OSIR Report for the Sales Department

SALES OSIR

Name: _____

Date: ___July 20_____

Objective:

Cust. Satisfaction: survey rating of >4   Priority 35%

Status:

Deliverables	Due Date	Status	Comments
1. Build Prototypes	Jan 31	Done	
2. Iterate Design	Feb 15	Done	
3. Robust Test	Mar 1	Done	
4. Qual. w/Platform	April 15	Not Done	See Qualification Test Results
5. Documentation	July 1	Not Done	Incomplete per guidelines
6. Exit Phase II	Aug 1		

Issues:

- Platform qualification rushed and inadequate, and documentation not complete.
- This is a set-up for a bad Alpha in Phase III, and puts us back on the familiar road to disappointing our customers. Let's do what we said we would do.

Recommendations:

- Back up and complete these steps of the PDP this week!
- Crash team from Engineering and Manufacturing for platform qualification.
- Crash team from Sales for support on documentation.

recommendations. The qualification piece was driven by Engineering but required Manufacturing's involvement. The documentation piece was also driven by Engineering but Sales had a keen interest and was offering increased support.

Issues will eventually become the exception rather than the rule, as people contributing to each objective develop clear expectations and begin to self-align around them. However, issues are inevitable in the initial stages of an organization-wide PS. The issue of not following the existing development process was just one of a number of problems that surfaced as the team conducted its first several OSIR reviews. As the consultant in this intervention observed, "the OSIR reviews acted as a guided missile launched into the heart of the company's problems and provided a safe way for the senior staff members to talk about their deepest hopes and fears." This may all sound very bleak, but is exactly what needs to happen for an organization to transcend hierarchical and organizational boundaries and organize around the work at hand.

Step 5. Reconfigure Resources

OBJECTIVE: Implement the work review decisions.

The staff's goal as they review OSIR reports is to make resource management decisions. These decisions focus on whether:

1. the organization's resources are being employed as expected,

2. the organization's resources need to be reallocated, and/or

3. plans need to be altered to fit the current availability and distribution of resources.

These are significantly different but equally relevant ways to frame the issues. Reconfiguring resources is just a term to summarize all three.

As the Etec management staff wrestled with the issue of the organization not following its own product development process, the focus centered on getting the resources employed as expected. Predictably, underneath the surface problem, there were not enough resources available. During the first year of implementation, the only way to allocate more resources to this critical project was to re-assign them from other projects running in parallel. This decision would be very unlikely to happen in organizations where each department "manages" itself independently. But because Etec made these tough decisions and reassigned resources, overall business performance improved significantly in 1997. The next time resources needed to be added, an infusion of new investor capital, earned by the company's recent success, was there to meet the need.

Figure 5.5	**Staff Level Self-Assessment Form**

Score the first 10 items from 1 to 5
    1 = not at all   5 = to a great extent

TO WHAT EXTENT DID WE...

1. link functional objectives to overall objectives?   _____

2. limit ourselves to 3-7 objectives?   _____

3. use goals that we were absolutely committed to?   _____

4. buy in to each other's objectives and goals?   _____

5. monitor progress to goals regularly throughout the period?   _____

6. use the OSIR format as intended?   _____

7. use performance data to support status reports?   _____

8. make decisions and take action on cross-functional issues?   _____

9. empower the leader to make decisions, and commit to those decisions?   _____

10. consult all team members before decisions were made?   _____

Assuming prior staff meetings were of medium effectiveness, how effective were our meetings during the last period?

1	**2**	**3**	**4**	**5**
Low		**Medium**		**High**

© 2001 The Center for Effective Performance, Inc.

Step 6. Conduct Self-Assessment and Document Results

OBJECTIVE: Help the client assess if PS conditions are present and working.

It is recommended that the client assess both their execution of the PS and the actual results achieved at the end of each planning period. Figure 5.5 shows a simple self-assessment form. Though results are usually apparent from the status charts presented throughout the process, it is important that the client look at the results as a whole. However, ensuring that the team takes the time to assess and, if appropriate, celebrate these results often takes some consultant coaching.

It is worthwhile to recall that the clients were initially quite suspicious of the process-oriented nature of the PS. They were more interested in solutions than a process. What they learned, however, was that in order to get solutions that would stick, they needed processes that would drive the

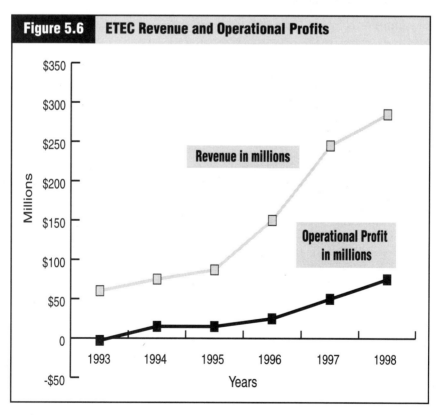

Figure 5.6   **ETEC Revenue and Operational Profits**

organization to develop solutions that they "owned." The consultant didn't provide any of the solutions, and as a result, those solutions were implemented in line with the organization's own plans and objectives.

By the end of 1996, the client asked the consultant to help them "own" the PS by providing them with training and coaching some internal facilitators. From that point on the consultant was used as kind of a "super-coach," returning periodically to assess progress and refresh practices as appropriate.

Figure 5.6 shows the overall long-term results of this PS intervention. This table is taken directly from Etec annual reports. During 1997, Etec took ownership for the PS. By 1998, it became apparent that Etec had achieved its goal of capitalizing on the semiconductor miniaturization. By this point they had become very attractive to key players in the semiconductor equipment industry and were acquired, at eight times their annual earnings.

These are the key steps to implementing the PS at the organization-wide level. As with the previous levels, the final step is to link to the other organizational levels. Now that we have seen how the PS is implemented at all organizational levels, we can proceed to the desired end result of this approach to performance consulting.

Linking It All Together: The Self-Sustaining Performance System

Step 7. Link to Cross-functional and Individual/Small Group Level

OBJECTIVE: Create a Self-Sustaining Performance System.

The senior staff at Etec spent a few months implementing the PS conditions on themselves before driving those conditions down into the organization (to the cross-functional and individual/small group levels). In reality, Etec couldn't resolve the most critical issues until the lower-level expectations aligned with the organization-wide plans and reliable performance data was being fed back up to the senior staff. For example, the issue of not following the existing development process was not fully resolved until that process had been put into a process-oriented PS which drove clear expectations at the individual and small group level. Although implementing a PS at the organization-wide level is an intervention in its own right, results like those achieved at Etec will not happen until core processes, projects, and most individuals are operating in the three PS conditions most of the time. Linking the PS's at all three levels of the organization gets our clients to the ultimate desired end result: a Self-Sustaining Performance System.

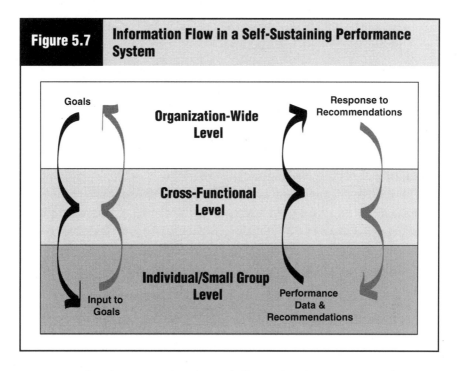

Figure 5.7   **Information Flow in a Self-Sustaining Performance System**

Figure 5.7 diagrams the desired flow of information in the Self-Sustaining Performance System. The general idea is for goals to flow downwards, and reliable performance data (self-monitored feedback) to flow upwards. Note how performance data from the individual/small group level informs decisions at the cross-functional level. Likewise, cross-functional level performance data informs decisions at the next level up. Remember that the pearl at the center of the organizational "onion" is commitment to performance goals. The only way to ensure that expectations are truly aligned and committed to is to allow each level in the organization to have input to those expectations. Also, communicating recommendations and requests upwards (for decisions requiring higher-level authority) is only worthwhile if the next level up responds to those recommendations.

The Etec case is one example where PS implementation began at the top of the organization and was then linked downward. There are some obvious benefits to starting at the top, but it is by no means required to be successful. At Raven University, for example, implementation began at the cross-functional level and migrated down to the individual/small group level, but has since also migrated upwards to the campus senior staff level. Likewise, in the aircraft parts case in chapter 2, the organization began by establishing individual level performance systems, but was then in the perfect position to expand the PS conditions upwards. The best place to begin a PS implementation depends on how the client organization frames its current challenges and opportunities. It also depends to some extent on how much the performance consultant is prepared to take on. As discussed in chapter 1, one of the benefits of a PS is that consulting at the lower levels in the organization builds the consultant's skills and confidence for consulting at higher levels in the organization.

The Self-Sustaining Performance System is an alternative approach to performance consulting that you can begin practicing immediately and puts any performance consultant in the position of *making an impact* with their clients.

Chapter 6 addresses a secondary but equally important objective of this book: to explore the implications of this approach on the role of training and performance professionals in organizations. How can training and performance departments position themselves to leverage the Self-Sustaining Performance System? What is the role of the internal SPS consultant?

Question & Answer

1. Does the term "organization-wide" always refer to starting at the most senior level of an enterprise?

Definitely not. It would be ideal to begin this level of implementation at the executive staff level, but this level is often not accessible to the performance consultant as a point of entry. The same basic approach applies to working with the senior level of management in any part of the organization that is accountable for its own profit and loss (e.g., the senior staff of any profit center within an enterprise). The approach has also been successful working with the staffs of factories and other large entities within a profit and loss center. But be aware that the further away from profit and loss responsibility, the more the overall goals of the entity will be outside the direct control of the managers of that entity. When this is the case, the overall goals of the target group can get changed without their input, and this can create frustration and implementation setbacks.

2. How long should each planning period be? How far out should performance plan objectives be set?

It depends. Performance planning is not strategic planning; it's about clarifying which accomplishments will be key to support a strategic plan or direction. Because the tactical planning structures of most organizations are set up on an annual basis, it is often convenient to align the performance planning cycle with that annual cycle. However, when an organization is initially implementing this approach, it sometimes makes sense to begin planning only six or nine months out. This abbreviated cycle can be an important advantage, in that the team will see how they performed against their plans sooner.

Performance plans are not intended to be written in stone. As external issues arise and performance data becomes available, the group can decide to add or remove objectives. In order to add new objectives, some existing objective(s) often need to be removed. In all cases, these changes should be noted during the self-assessment stage and considered when creating the next period plans.

3. In the case study you mention the staff "reaching agreement," but what if the staff members don't agree on everything?

Part of the consultant's job is to coach the decision-making body (at whatever level) on consultative decision-making. One of the key principles of consultative decision-making is "disagree and commit" (Daniels, 1997). When the team empowers a decision maker, each individual team member is agreeing up front that he or she will commit to future decisions, even ones he or she doesn't personally think are the best decisions. This doesn't mean that everyone is emotionally comfortable with all decisions, but that they will support them anyway. Question 4 below addresses the problem of resistance to consultative decision-making.

4. What if all staff members don't agree that the performance system approach should become a way of doing business? Is there ever resistance to the overall approach?

In the Etec case and others, there have been team members who did not buy in to some aspects of the PS approach. The approach often raises issues that some individuals may be uncomfortable facing. Some managers are much more comfortable operating in a situation where the tough cross-functional issues don't ever get raised. Ultimately, the PS approach will not survive if team members are not willing to provide performance data, let issues surface, and buy in to the consultative decision-making process. A choice becomes apparent: either the team lets those who don't see the value kill the intervention, or those who don't see the value are encouraged to leave. As the consultant, it is good to recognize and call out these group dynamics, but the choice of whether to continue the intervention always belongs to the client.

5. Doesn't implementing an SPS alter the entire culture of the organization?

The implementation of the SPS will certainly require a culture change on the part of the vast majority of client organizations. One of Bill Daniels' observations which has played out in my experience is that true cultural changes can take at least three years to happen.

I personally have not found it necessary to approach the initial PS intervention (especially at the individual/small group and cross-functional levels) as a cultural change. In my opinion, the best time to raise the issue of culture change is after there are some measurable improvements in performance and the benefits of expanding the intervention are becoming apparent. Part of the power of this approach, I believe, comes from getting effective behaviors into place and then letting the client discover the principles behind the behaviors. They become very interested in the principles after they see results.

CHAPTER 6

LEADING THE CHARGE: TRANSITIONING TO A SELF-SUSTAINING PERFORMANCE SYSTEM

As was suggested in the Introduction, training and performance improvement functions have an opportunity to expand their influence in organizations. "Opportunity," however, may not be the appropriate word. In *Achieving Desired Business Results* (1999), Tony O'Driscoll aptly describes where the training function in organizations has come from, and where it is almost assuredly going. He makes a convincing and well-researched case that the role of the training function is changing, whether training organizations drive that change or not. He summarizes these changes in figure 6.1 on the next page.

My suggestion that the training and performance profession has the opportunity to follow in the footsteps of the finance and information technology professions is supported by the third transition. Now that "human capital" is recognized by business managers as a competitive tool, performance improvement technology is *bound* to emerge as a competitive resource. But the transition that is even more supportive of the emergence of a Self-Sustaining Performance System is the fourth one: that organizations are moving towards "an integrated performance improvement

Figure 6.1	"Five Major Transitions That Will Impact Training"
FROM	**TO**
Learning as an end in itself	Valued performance as the primary measure of effectiveness
Training and other interventions as tactical responses to somewhat larger tactical problems	Performance technology as a strategic response to strategic needs relating to people and productivity
A view of training as overhead and support, susceptible to budget cutting and downsizing	Performance technology as a competitive resource, perhaps even important during business downturns
Interventions placed in HR functional chimneys that do not communicate with one another	An integrated performance improvement system that is systemic throughout the organization
A focus on educational results, e.g., learning	A focus on organizational learning and business results, e.g., the bottom line

Used with the permission of the International Society for Performance Improvement. Copyright 1999.

system that is systemic throughout the organization." O'Driscoll identifies several successful companies that are already moving in this direction. In the high-performance work system, as O'Driscoll calls it, performers "are expected to assume ownership of the process or problem and to improve the process over time."

This brings us back to the parable at the beginning of chapter 1. While some old-world business managers still look to the hard-working oracles in their training functions as people on whom to unload and forget about training problems, forward-thinking business managers are demanding something else. They realize that to fully utilize the organization's human capital, all levels of the organization must be engaged in performance improvement all the time. Contributing to systemic improvement (as opposed to everyone constantly tweaking their isolated pieces of the whole) must be the expectation for every member of the organization. In today's globally competitive environment, organizations that do not practice systemic performance improvement will be under constant siege, and ultimately they will be "sacked."

The challenge for the training and performance function is to help move organizations towards systemic performance improvement without taking responsibility for organizational performance. I believe a big part of the answer is a Self-Sustaining Performance System. But questions remain. How does the training and performance function set itself up to facilitate a Self-Sustaining Performance System? What is the role of the training and performance department when responsibility for excellent performance is owned by each performer? What is the role of the internal performance consultant and where does this capability fit into the larger organization?

Defining these roles is a performance challenge in itself, and there is never one best approach to a performance challenge. The intention here is not to define the one best structure of the training and performance function (remember the caution in chapter 1 about over-design). Rather, the intention is to suggest a number of ways that the training and performance function can be a catalyst rather than a pawn in the transition to systemic performance improvement. Change requires leadership, and so most of the advice in this chapter is directed primarily at training and performance managers. This is partially because the training manager decides how training and performance resources will be utilized. If you are not a manager, however, this information can still be useful as you find a way to communicate these ideas to the training manager in your organization. It will be the training managers (or whomever is responsible for training and performance improvement in the organization) who determine whether the training and performance function is a driver or bystander in the transition to systemic performance improvement.

Generalist and Specialist Roles

There will always be a need for people who specialize in training delivery, training development and even specific aspects of training development (e.g., instructional design, technology-based development, performance support, etc.), but systemic performance improvement creates the need for generalists as well. The generalist performance consultant needs to be, and be viewed, more like a general management consultant. As I've demonstrated, management is largely misunderstood by organizations, and someone who understands it well is in an excellent position to build credibility and make an impact in the organization. The most effective performance consultants will be those who have the Performance System perspective on management, have performance analysis skills, and are literate in a variety of performance improvement specialties. Many experienced training and performance professionals already possess the latter two, but how will they get the opportunity to implement Performance Systems?

A good place to begin is to let selected individuals respond to incoming client requests from a Performance System perspective. Client managers often come to the training department with a request for training on a specific task or job function. They are looking for relatively simple solutions, not lengthy and detailed analyses. Utilizing the individual/small group PS implementation flowchart, the internal performance consultant can perform an informal PS audit, help establish clear expectations and self-monitored feedback, and facilitate measurable performance results within a couple of weeks (less time than it often takes to implement training). During the "control of resources" step (step 6 in the flowchart), the generalist can coach the client group to identify additional barriers to success. Training may come up at this stage, and the generalist can pass that request to a training specialist. If the top barrier identified by the client group has to do with faulty software, that issue would be passed on to a specialist in the appropriate support organization. As a generalist, the performance consultant would stay involved with the client group until they were performing to agreed upon expectations.

When the developing performance consultant is comfortable expanding his or her impact, it is time to approach the cross-functional level. At this stage, rather than just responding to requests, the performance consultant can go after process and project problems in which client managers wouldn't necessarily expect the training department to take the lead. In chapter 3, an accounts receivable problem presented an opportunity for a process-oriented PS. In chapter 4, it was the typical inability to achieve project schedule and quality goals when developing strategic products. Interested members of your organization will pick this up faster than you think, because although the perceived problems vary, implementing an SPS always involves roughly the same steps. Every individual/small group PS implemented will provide lessons learned for cross-functional level performance systems.

Having generalists in the department will also expand the influence of everyone in the group. How often do we hear frustrated trainers grumbling because management sees every performance problem as a training problem, or because the client sees no value in follow-up or evaluation? As performance consultants guide the client organization towards a systemic approach, the client group will learn why performance improvement is systemic in nature. This helps them see the value in performance analysis, follow-up and measuring the impact of specific changes. Educated clients will be more sophisticated in their utilization of dedicated training and performance resources. They will also be more likely to partner on performance issues, rather than jumping to conclusions (such as assuming every problem is a training problem). The generalist and specialist roles in the training department can and should be complementary in implementing an SPS.

If your training department has only a few dedicated resources, it makes even more sense to develop some or all of those resources into generalists. What is a more effective way to utilize limited training and performance resources? Having them drive training and performance in a few isolated places, or having them facilitate systemic performance improvement in the organization's core projects and processes? The latter certainly enables you to make a larger impact on the client organization. If systemic performance improvement happens to drive the need for more specialist training resources (internal or outsourced), it will be clear to the client organization why those resources are needed and how they will impact organizational performance.

The Training Manager as Performance Consultant

The training manager is usually the one person with the most access to, and influence over, the decision-makers of the larger organization. Sitting on the management staff of the organization is one of the best ways to influence how the organization views ongoing performance. Once you have developed one or more generalist performance consultants, you can speed up the transition by introducing the management staff to the organization-wide Performance System described in chapter 5.

One way to accomplish this is for the training manager to play the role that was played by the external consultant in the case study. The key components of that role were to:

- Develop and be able to articulate a vision of the Self-Sustaining Performance System.

- Coach the leader of the management staff to champion the implementation (again, the training function should not take responsibility for this transition).

- Coach the management staff to use the simple tools (performance plans, OSIR's, etc.) and to conduct consultative decision-making.

- Guide the management staff through the steps in the flowchart (figure 5.1), including taking performance systems to the middle and lower organizational levels.

A slight variation would be for the training manager to have one of the newly developed generalist performance consultants perform this role. This would alleviate the need for the training manager to play both the facilitator and "staff member" role at the same time (which is possible, but not easy). If the Performance System takes hold at the senior staff level, there will soon be demand to drive the system down into the organization so that accurate performance data is flowing up to the staff. This is another reason why it is recommended to begin the transition to systemic performance improvement from the bottom up.

Leveraging Management Development

Because a Self-Sustaining Performance System is so closely related to effective management, management development can be another important part of transitioning to systemic performance improvement. Any of the four types of PS implementation described in chapters 2–5 can be turned into educational resources for managers at different levels in the organization. But just sharing the principles will probably not be enough to drive the transition to systemic performance improvement.

In 1994, when I was asked to lead the transition (as an HRD initiative) at a large semiconductor manufacturer, the company had already been putting all of its first-line managers through a one-day course on the individual/small group PS. However, when we looked for managers who had actually implemented a PS, we found only four. Interestingly, each of those examples was a documentable success story. After investigating why so few managers followed through, we began a three-pronged approach to increase the transfer of training from the classroom to the workplace.

First, we expanded the training itself. The one-day course had high ratings (people appreciated it), but it didn't provide much guidance or any practice designing a PS. In the expanded course, managers saw examples of successful Performance Systems from the same company, were given time and guidance to design a PS specific to their work team, and then received feedback on those initial designs. The second prong was reinforcement and recognition. In the course, managers were told that there would be follow-up to see which individuals were able to implement their PS. Managers who were successful would be invited to come back to the training (which was always held at a nice offsite location) and share their stories. The organization also published the success stories in an internal web-based document which was incorporated into the course. Optional personal coaching was the third prong. Managers could sign up to have a coach meet with them several times after the training to provide further guidance on designing and implementing their PS.

In a study of over 300 managers who participated in this revised intervention, the number that actually implemented a PS went up dramatically. The success stories were all documented and used to encourage hundreds more participants after that. This particular example of using management development to support the transition to systemic performance improvement is documented in detail elsewhere (Esque and McCausland, 1997).

There is also no rule against teaching the Performance System to individual contributors. I have seen good results from teaching the individual/small group PS to intact teams. It is important to note, however, that the decision to work in a PS is a decision for management and not for the individual contributors. There is an important and subtle distinction here. The PS conditions work best when the performers are committed to the performance expectations, and performers should have a say in the development of performance goals. But it is perfectly okay for management to require performers to work in a PS. The PS sets individuals (and hence the organization) up for success, and it is not up to each individual to decide if the organization should strive for success.

Getting Out from Under the "Training Hat"

Having explored a number of ways to get the transition to systemic performance improvement started, a challenge should be recognized. Despite signs that the transition is imminent, it is not a given that business managers will look to the training department as key players in this transition. For most of the past 50 years, organizations have looked to the training department (and hence any dedicated training and performance resources) to administer training. Training departments have evolved a great deal, but the utilization of training departments hasn't kept up. Business managers do not necessarily view the training department as the resident experts on organizational performance. For this reason, it may be challenging for the generalist performance consultant role to "take hold" while residing in the training department.

During the ten years I spent in various internal training capacities, I couldn't help but notice an interesting trend. The more closely my clients associated me with training, the less I was able to impact measurable performance improvement. When I was perceived as a trainer, I was only expected to administer training (which was often worthy, but also limiting). I was able to test this theory on a couple of occasions in which internal clients mistakenly viewed me as something other than a trainer.

On one occasion I had developed training on manufacturing inventory management for a factory. Somehow, a different factory came under the impression that I was an inventory management consultant who had been instrumental in helping the original factory. That was not the case; however, I was asked to come in and consult on inventory management (including implementing the training course). The course went well, but importantly, I was able to influence the manufacturing organization to alter their entire goal-setting process to achieve the goals of inventory management. Their numbers also went up, and the factory was allowed to keep producing despite a scheduled shut-down.

On another occasion I was in a training and performance department, but the name of the department was rather misleading, so my internal clients usually didn't know what my title was. This gave me the opportunity to help guide my first project-oriented PS. When that implementation led to improved product time to market, I was asked to help a number of other organizations, and my performance consulting career had begun.

I will not go so far as to say the generalist performance consultant cannot be successful as a member of training, but it can sometimes be easier from a position outside the training or performance improvement department. Here are a couple of examples of other approaches that led to opportunities to implement an SPS. One colleague became the "technical assistant" of a senior executive, doing everything from writing speeches and screening e-mail to ensuring there were advance agendas for meetings and facilitating executive staff meetings. The latter two responsibilities, in particular, provide excellent leverage for performance consulting using an SPS. Another colleague has a small OD department and reports directly to his general manager. Because he sits on the organization's senior staff, he is always present when key decisions are made, and he has had the opportunity to structure those staff meetings around an organization-wide PS (which is now moving rapidly towards an SPS).

If training and performance professionals are going to play a role in the transition, they must consider the history associated with the training department. Part of the solution may be in renaming what has historically been called the training function. As an interim step, those interested in becoming performance consultants might explore roles that report outside the training department. I would encourage training managers to do what it takes to support the development and acceptance of performance consultants, even if it means placing them elsewhere for the time being.

Partnering with External Consultants

A related tactic is to bring in PS expertise from the outside, in the form of external consultants. In the capacity of external consultant, I am constantly asked to help transfer knowledge of the SPS and supporting skills to internal resources so that the SPS can continue to thrive without me. I'm quite convinced that it is in the interest of both the client organization and the consultant to help clients achieve an SPS. The benefit for the organization is excellent performance and, in my experience, the benefit for the consultant is often follow-up work and referrals. As a result, I am able to spend the majority of my time consulting rather than marketing.

External consultants probably also have an advantage in leading changes that impact an organization's culture. As they say, it is hard to be a prophet in your own land. I personally had good luck riding on the coattails of external consultants in order to create internal performance consulting opportunities for myself. Now that I am on the other side of the fence, I always look for opportunities to return the favor and set up internal resources for success. I suspect that other external performance consultants have a similar perspective.

At the moment, there is a shortage of consultants who are helping organizations implement systemic performance improvement. I believe this is because a different model of consulting has been dominant for so long. The dominant model has been the "throw another log on the fire" approach. Log throwing, remember, is the approach in which the consultant (or support group) takes responsibility for making the problem go away, reports back on the short-term results, and then moves on to build another fire. Meanwhile, the performance that had been "fixed" predictably drifts back to where it was. It has to, because the "default" performance system in place supports that performance. Without systemic change, an awful lot of energy is spent making very little lasting change.

Conclusion: Let's Stop Throwing Logs

To recap, in this chapter I've provided ideas to help the training and performance function begin to facilitate the transition of organizations to systemic performance improvement. There is reason to believe that the transition will be an emerging trend in organizations, and who better to provide the catalyst than training and performance improvement professionals?

Think of the potential impact if client managers only interacted with training and performance resources who could articulate the systemic issues that prevent effective organizational performance. A slight adjustment to their management approach could create a whole new level of effectiveness. What if the majority of managers were striving to get and keep their teams working in an SPS? What if every process and project team constantly tracked its own performance and anticipated and prevented cross-functional problems? What if the senior staff of every organization spent most of their time discussing progress against goals, and what they needed to do *now* to best support the members of their organization to achieve those goals? Organizational performance would improve systemically from here on out. The possibilities indicate a future for our field that will allow training and performance professionals to have a significant impact in organizations.

I began by expressing my belief that members of organizations, like all other individuals, like to be and feel valued. We want our profession to be able to impact the business world positively. An SPS enables that to take place. I encourage all training and performance professionals and all organizations to investigate the Self-Sustaining Performance System. The impact could be enormous.

Question & Answer

1. Okay, I'm interested. Where do I (and/or my organization) begin?

Building this capability can occur one individual at a time (as individual professionals look to expand their personal influence) or it can occur an organization at a time. Some of you will want more information and more examples before you begin. Start by referring to the resources listed in the response to question 2. Others will probably rather just jump right in. One important piece of advice was already provided in chapter 1—peel the onion from the inside out. Find an individual or a small group that is frustrated with current performance and do an informal Performance System audit. Chances are you will find that expectations are not clear, and the performer or small group is not generating self-monitored feedback. Then help get these conditions in place. It is often very informative to practice this on yourself first, in regards to one of your important tasks/roles.

There are many benefits to an organization taking on a new capability all at the same time. Its members can design the capability into their strategies and processes, organize themselves into generalist and specialist roles, and reinforce each other's behavior. Likewise, one of the best ways to begin to learn about the PS would be for a training and performance department to implement the approach on itself at all levels. This way you not only experience implementing the principles, but also what it feels like to work within the principles on a daily and weekly basis. Remember that the pearl at the center of the performance onion is commitment. If you and/or your organization are serious about making an impact, the first step is to commit yourself (or your department) to doing so.

Question & Answer

2. Where can I get more specific information on how to implement a Self-Sustaining Performance System?

The table below identifies where to find more information about specific topics discussed in this book:

TOPIC	PUBLICATIONS
Individual and small group level Performance Systems	*Breakthrough Performance: Managing for Speed and Flexibility* by William R. Daniels. Mill Valley, CA: ACT Publishing, 1995.
Project-oriented cross-functional level Performance Systems	*No Surprises Project Management: A Proven Early Warning System for Staying on Track* by Timm J. Esque. Mill Valley, CA: ACT Publishing, 1999.
Organization-wide Performance Systems	*Change-ABLE Organization: Key Management Practices for Speed and Flexibility* by William R. Daniels. Mill Valley, CA: ACT Publishing, 1997.
Closely related approaches to management and consulting	*The Great Game of Business* by Jack Stack with Bo Burlingham. New York, NY: Currency Doubleday, 1992.
	The Breakthrough Strategy: Using Short Term Successes to Build the High Performance Organization by Robert H. Schaffer. New York, NY: Harper Collins, 1988.

BUILDING RESPECT

A SELF-SUSTAINING PERFORMANCE SYSTEM IS both a high-leverage tool for improving organizational performance and a vehicle for becoming a valued performance consultant. But there is a third benefit that drives me to continue to develop and share this approach. I believe that the SPS builds mutual respect among those who operate in it. I agree with Don Tosti (1998) that "true respect has little to do with showing deference to 'betters'. Rather, it means behaving toward others in a way that assumes they have value: that differences stem from legitimate motives, and that people will typically behave responsibly." This building of mutual respect further increases the capability of the organization to succeed, but I also believe it is important in its own right. Members of an organization who learn to interact with the assumption of mutual respect are not only more valuable team members, they are also more valuable members of society.

This claim may seem a little puzzling because up until now the term mutual respect hasn't even been mentioned. In fact, in my consulting practice, I usually don't bring up the issue of mutual respect until a client is well into the Performance System, if at all. My clients are not looking or asking for increased mutual respect, they are looking and asking for solutions to their immediate business problems (and for tools to sustain excellent performance). The PS gives them both; it addresses both immediate solutions and long-term systemic improvement. It also builds mutual respect as a natural byproduct.

The Erosion and Restoration of Mutual Respect

How do we know that our client organizations aren't already swimming in mutual respect? One very large hint is the cross-functional finger-pointing that's part of the vicious cycle mentioned earlier in the book. I have yet to come across a cross-functional entity that is under any real pressure to perform that does not have evidence of finger-pointing. Let's examine this very common phenomenon.

Cross-functional finger-pointing is occurring whenever members of one functional group accuse members of a different group of not holding up their end of the bargain. The inherent assumption here is based on blame: that a member of another group prevented other individuals from fulfilling their goals. If the assumption was more respectful, the observations would be more like the following: that something in the system failed, and the end result was that individuals didn't get what they needed to be successful. But what I hear from members of struggling teams is much more like the former than the latter.

In my experience, many functional teams are failing to provide what other teams need (when they need it) in order to be successful. However, I have yet to find any evidence that groups are intentionally failing. And in fact, when we set up conditions where these same groups have absolute clarity in what needs to be delivered, plus ample input into the schedule and resources required to deliver it, they always succeed in delivering in the future.

So why would anyone assume that someone else is deliberately performing at a level below their capability? One reason is because they are afraid of being accused of the same. Poor management (which can easily arise even under the stewardship of very capable managers) sets people up for failure. But if management isn't properly understood, people will assume that performers are to blame for poor performance. When a process or project goes bad, somebody is going to get blamed, and the best way to avoid that blame is to point fingers in another direction—any direction. So finger-pointing begins as a form of protection. But if it is allowed to persist, the accusations become a part of the accuser's belief system. After spending lots of time in any environment of ineffective management, it becomes a basic assumption that "they" are setting "us" up for failure, sometimes even before two groups have ever worked together.

Finger-pointing at the cross-functional level is probably the most openly talked about symptom of organizations operating without effective Performance Systems. But the same dynamic exists at the individual/small group level, as well as at the organization-wide level where the players are senior staff members. Ineffective management also isn't the only structure that supports and encourages this dynamic. One example is forced distribution performance appraisal systems, where someone always has to be labeled "unsuccessful." Another is zero-sum budgeting, where the only way to increase "our" budget dollars is to get some of "their" budget dollars. And there are others. These structures are not necessarily wrong, but when they are not balanced with the Performance System, they lead to an erosion of mutual respect that is reflected in both individual and organizational performance.

If ineffective management and some of our common organizational structures erode mutual respect, how does an SPS restore it? The answer gets down to two basic assumptions behind the Self-Sustaining Performance System.

1. There is no one best way to achieve a specific result.

Accusations of failure or success are simply judgment calls until the appropriate people agree on the desired end result and how to know if it has been achieved. Getting that agreement is called "clarifying expectations," and this is the first step to implementing a Performance System. At all levels of implementation, a Performance System requires absolute clarity of expectations (the end result) and absolute flexibility about methods to achieve the results (within policy and legal boundaries, of course). A big part of building respect is helping people to suspend their assumptions about how something should be done, and focus instead on whether the desired result is being achieved.

Mutual respect increases when individuals and teams who are dependent on each other start reliably meeting their expectations. Just as importantly, when clear performance expectations are made public and performers have reliable data about their progress against those expectations, the performers will be the first ones to point out if they are not going to be successful. Unless other existing structures prevent it, they will ask for help in time for something to be done. This "early warning" builds respect because it becomes apparent that those asking for help care about the later steps in the process/project. Also, when these early warnings are based on data and communicated effectively, it becomes apparent exactly why help will be needed, which is almost always due to environmental factors and not a lack of skill or motivation on the part of the performers. The focus can move from blaming others to figuring out what adjustments can be made to stay on track

2. The only real control is self-control.

Having clear goals and reliable data about performance against the goals creates the opportunity to adjust or self-correct. But acting on that information—making the decision on how to self-correct and owning implementation of the correction—is self-control, and is what allows performers to have a sense of control. Some managers and some support groups believe that they can make these decisions for the performers and control their performance. To the extent that the performers also believe they can be controlled, this belief system will perpetuate itself. But these beliefs run counter to the Self-Sustaining Performance System, and one individual or group trying to control the behavior or performance of others rarely achieves the intended result.

On the other hand, expecting performers to take responsibility for making and implementing self-correction (improvement) decisions increases both their self-respect and their sense of control. This does not mean providing unlimited authority to individual contributors, but rather expecting performers to drive the problem-solving and decision-making process. In the SPS approach, management maintains ultimate responsibility for decisions regarding the organization's overall goals, but those decisions are based on bottom-up performance data and recommendations, and the decisions are carried out by the people closest to the work. I know of no better way to build respect between managers and performers, or of optimizing the chances of achieving desired results.

I am intrigued by the possibility that building mutual respect within organizations just might spill over into people's everyday lives. As I said in the Introduction, people like to be appreciated by others, and the same is true within an organization. To respect others, even before they've had a chance to "earn it," is to appreciate others.

—*Timm J. Esque*

Endnotes

Chapter One

1. As you probably know, the term oracle can be used to refer to a deity or soothsayer sought out for advice, the advice given, or the place where the deity or soothsayer resides, such as Delphi. The concept of an oracle "staffing up" is apparently not far-fetched: "During Delphi's busy heyday, in the 500's B.C., as many as three [soothsayers] held the office at once" (Sacks, 1995).

Chapter Two

1. Dale Brethower, Geary Rummler, and others at the University of Michigan Bureau of Industrial Relations developed and taught the concept of a human performance system beginning in 1965. See Brethower (1982) and Rummler and Brache (1990) for their descriptions of the performance system applied to the business environment.

Chapter Three

1. Brethower (1982) also calls out the importance of cross-functional coordination (he used the term interlocking job models).

References

Beniger, James R. *The Control Revolution: Technological and Economic Origins of the Information Society*. Cambridge: Harvard University Press, 1987.

Block, Stanley B. and Hirt, Geoffrey A. *Foundations of Financial Management*. Homewood, IL: Irwin, 1989.

Brooks, Frederick P. Jr. *The Mythical Man-Month: Essays on Software Engineering*. Reading, MA: Addison-Wesley, 1975.

Brethower, Dale M. "The classroom as a self-modifying system." Ph.D. diss., University of Michigan, 1970.

Brethower, Dale M. "The Total Performance System." *In Industrial Behavior Modification*, edited by R.M. O'Brien, A.M. Dickenson, and M.P. Rosow. New York: Pergamon Press, 1982.

Butman, John. *Juran: A Lifetime of Influence*. New York: John Wiley and Sons, Inc., 1997.

Daniels, William R. *Breakthrough Performance: Managing for Speed and Flexibility*. Mill Valley, CA: ACT Publishing, 1995.

Daniels, William R. *Change-ABLE Organization: Key Practices for Speed and Flexibility*. Mill Valley, CA: ACT Publishing, 1997.

Deterline, William A. "Feedback Systems." In *Handbook of Human Performance Technology*, edited by H.D. Stolovitch and E.J. Keeps. San Francisco : Jossey-Bass, 1992.

Emery Air Freight. *Behaviorism and the Bottom Line.* Training film about Edward J. Feeney's productivity improvement study, 1973.

Esque, Timm J., ed. *The Breakthrough Systems Sampler.* Chandler, AZ: Intel Corporation in-house pub., 1996.

Esque, Timm J. *No Surprises Project Management: A Proven Early Warning System for Staying On Track.* Mill Valley, CA: ACT Publishing, 1999.

Esque, Timm J. and McCausland, Joel. "Taking Ownership for Transfer: A Management Development Case Study." *Performance Improvement Quarterly* 10, no. 2, 1997.

Gilbert, Thomas F. *Human Competence: Engineering Worthy Performance.* New York: McGraw Hill, 1978.

Glasser, William. *The Control Theory Manager.* New York: HarperCollins, 1994.

Goodgame, Dan. "The Game of Risk: How the Best Golfer in the World Got Even Better." *Time Magazine* 156, no. 7 (August 14, 2000).

Gup, Benton E. *Principles of Financial Management.* New York: John Wiley and Sons, 1987.

Juran, J.M. *Managerial Breakthrough.* New York: McGraw Hill, 1964.

Mager, Robert F. and Pipe, Peter. *Analyzing Performance Problems.* 3rd ed. Atlanta: The Center for Effective Performance, Inc., 1997.

McGregor, Douglas. *The Human Side of Enterprise.* Boston: McGraw Hill, 1960.

Miller, G.A., Galanter, E., and Pribram, K.H. *Plans and the Structure of Behavior.* New York: Adams-Bannister-Cox, 1960.

O'Driscoll, Tony. *Achieving Desired Business Results: A Framework for Developing Human Performance Technology in Organizations.* Washington DC: International Society for Performance Improvement, 1999.

Pinchot, Gifford and Pinchot, Elizabeth. *The End of Bureaucracy and the Rise of the Intelligent Organization.* San Francisco: Berret-Koehler Publishers, 1993.

Rummler, Geary A. and Brache, Alan P. *Improving Performance: How to Manage the White Space on the Organization Chart*. San Francisco : Jossey-Bass Publishers, 1990.

Rychlak, Joseph F. *Discovering Free Will and Personal Responsibility*. Oxford: Oxford University Press, 1979.

Sacks, David. *Dictionary of the Ancient Greek World*. New York: Oxford University Press, 1997.

Scherr, Allan. "Managing for Breakthroughs in Productivity." *Human Resource Management* 28, no. 3, 1989.

Senge, Peter M. *The Fifth Discipline: The Art and Practice of the Learning Organization*. New York: Doubleday Currency, 1990.

Tosti, Donald T. "Partnering." Sausalito, CA: Vanguard Consulting, Inc., Working Paper #14, 1998.

Tosti, Donald T. "Systemic Change." Performance Improvement 39, no. 3, 2000.

Weiner, Norbert. *The Human Use of Human Beings: Cybernetics and Society*. Garden City, NY: Doubleday, 1954.

Index

Join ISPI Today!

International Society for Performance Improvement (ISPI) *is the leading international association of professionals who are dedicated to improving individual, organizational and societal performance.*

ISPI members hold management and line positions in performance technology, employee training, human resource development, instructional design, organizational development and other key management areas.

For four decades, ISPI members have been steadily improving performance for the largest, most successful organizations in some 40 countries around the World.

Individual ISPI members are employed by private firms and corporations (including 75% of the Fortune 100), leading educational institutions, non-profit organizations, and numerous city, state and provincial governments, as well as national civilian and military agencies of countries around the World.

ISPI corporate members and supporters include Arthur Andersen, CADDI, Comcast Cable, Eli Lilly, Ford Motor Company, Georgia-Pacific, Hewlett Packard, IBM, iGeneration, International Monetary Fund, Maritz, Metropolitan Life Insurance, Microsoft, Sun Microsystems, United States Coast Guard, United States Food and Drug Administration, Walgreen, Wells Fargo and others.

ISPI offers its members performance improvement education and networking through conferences, institutes, book publishing, professional journals, an interactive Website, research, and local chapters.

For more information about ISPI:

International Society for Performance Improvement
1400 Spring Street, Suite 260
Silver Spring, Maryland 20910 USA
Telephone: 1.301.587.8570
Fax: 1.301.587.8573
E-mail: info@ispi.org
Web: www.ispi.org

Experience ISPI...Experience Value!

Name _____

Title _____

Organization _____

Mailing Address _____

City _____

State/Province _____

Zip/Post Code _____

Country _____

Phone _____

Fax _____

E-mail _____

Credit Card # _____

❏ VISA ❏ MasterCard ❏ AMEX

Exp. Date _____

Signature _____

Membership Fees　　　　　　**$ US**

If you are outside the US or Canada, please see the supplemental postage charges below.

Active Member (includes $69 for PI)	$ 145	$
Student Member (Attach proof of full-time student status.)	$ 60	$
Retired Member	$ 60	$
Patron Member	$1,400	$
Sustaining Member	$ 950	$

Special New Member Offer

The Handbook of Human Performance Technology (Regularly $84.95)	$ 70	$

Subscription charges

Performance Improvement Quarterly (PIQ)		
Active Member	$ 40	$
Student/Retired Member	$ 22	$
Commercial/Library Subscription	$ 64	$
Performance Improvement (PI)		
Non-Member Subscription	$ 69	$
Commercial/Library Subscription	$ 69	$

Supplemental Postage Charges

Members and *PI* Subscribers Outside USA or Canada	$ 50	$
PIQ Subscribers Outside USA or Canada	$ 20	$

Your Total Investment　$ _____

MORE GREAT BOOKS FROM CEP PRESS

CEP Press is a full-service publisher of performance improvement, training, and management books and tools. All of our publications boast the same high quality and value, and the same practical resources and relevant information that you have come to expect from our worldwide renowned publications. **Order your copies today and get resources you'll use for a lifetime.**

	Quantity	Price	Total
Making an Impact: Building a Top-Performing Organization from the Bottom Up by Timm J. Esque **($16.95 US, $24.95 CAN)**			
Conquering Organizational Change: How to Succeed Where Most Companies Fail by Pierre Mourier & Martin Smith, Ph.D. **($18.95 US, $28.95 CAN)**			
The Business of Winning: A Manager's Guide to Building a Championship Team by Robert Evangelista **($18.95 US, $28.95 CAN)**			
Analyzing Performance Problems: How to figure out why people aren't doing what they should be, and what to do about it 3rd edition by Robert F. Mager & Peter Pipe **($19.95 US, $29.95 CAN)**			
Preparing Instructional Objectives: A critical tool in the development of effective instruction 3rd edition by Robert F. Mager **($19.95 US, $29.95 CAN)**			
Goal Analysis: How to clarify your goals so you can actually achieve them 3rd edition by Robert F. Mager **($19.95 US, $29.95 CAN)**			
Subtotal			
Shipping & Handling			
GA residents add 7% sales tax to the subtotal plus S&H. Canada and TX residents add applicable sales tax to the subtotal plus S&H.			
TOTAL ORDER			

U.S. Shipping & Handling: Please add $6 for the first book plus $1.50 for each additional book. Please allow four weeks for delivery by ground delivery.

Name _____

Phone _____ **Fax** _____

Organization _____

Address _____

City _____ **State** _____ **ZIP** _____

❏ My check for $_____ is enclosed.

Charge my ❏ Visa ❏ Mastercard ❏ AmEx Exp. Date _____

Card Number _____

Name on Card _____

Please send this form and your check or credit card number to:
CEP, P.O. Box 102462, Atlanta, GA 30368-2462

Call 1-800-558-4CEP for volume discount information and for shipping charges on international orders. For credit card orders, fax this order for faster delivery to (770) 458-9109 or use our Web site: www.ceppress.com